In-tensional

Intensional: from the Latin word *intênsiõ*, meaning to have strong feeling or tension between two people, objects or ideas.

In-tensional

A way forward for the church

Justin Duckworth

Alan Jamieson

Philip
Garside
Publishing Ltd.

Paperback International edition 2024:
ISBN 9781991027771

Also available

New Zealand paperback: ISBN 9781991027764
Paperback print-on-demand USA:
ISBN 9798325613944

PDF: ISBN 9781991027788
ePub / Kindle / Mobi: ISBN 9781991027795

Philip Garside Publishing Ltd
PO Box 17160
Wellington 6147
New Zealand

sales@philipgarsidebooks.com
www.philipgarsidebooks.com

Cover design and illustrations:
Grace Finnigan & Matthew Watson – Vine Design Trust

Contents

Acknowledgements

We particularly want to thank Colin, Sophie and Kelly who read the text and offered great insights and improvements. Thanks to Grace and Matt who designed the illustrations and book cover. We also thank Philip Garside for his work preparing and publishing this book.

Alan is deeply grateful to the community leaders at South West Baptist whose courage and leadership inspired his thinking and writing.

Justin says that this book would never have happened without Alan's encouragement (and organisation); for which he is very thankful. Likewise, huge thanks to St John's College Trust Board for resourcing the study that eventually led to In-tensional being published. To all those involved in Urban Vision, you continue to be a daily inspiration. To the whole Diocese of Wellington, your courage in living out centre-edge tension is phenomenal. Justin also sends a big mihi to his mates Nick, Phil, Martin and Alison. And of course arohanui to all his family.

Introduction

Getting on the Same Page

We've written this book because the western world is in crisis: a crisis of bewilderment and confusion and a loss of believable movements of hope. Many are crying out for help, help that we passionately believe is to be found in the life of Jesus and his church. And yet, at this opportune moment when the world is seeking answers, the church in the west is haemorrhaging people, has lost its compelling voice in our culture and shows little sign of gospel life or Kingdom hope. Despite this desperate situation, we see signs of life re-emerging within the body of Christ that can bring deep hope. These signs are desperately and urgently calling us to respond! Before we unpack this hope, let us introduce ourselves.

Justin is Anglican Bishop of what is arguably the most secular diocese in the world, but he is also a multidecadal intentional missional leader. Alan was senior pastor of one of the bigger and most well-known mission minded churches in New Zealand. He is also a sociologist of religion who twenty years ago was writing books on church decline and the faith of church leavers.

We are not here to bash churches, state the obvious about people leaving the church, or repeat the content of other church decline books. While we have both studied theology, church history and sociology in depth, this is not a theory book. Nor does it rehash the emergent forms of church variously described as missional, intentional, emergent, fresh expressions or alternative church. This is something quite different. We want to introduce an in-tensional conversation with traditional church leaders and structures and new forms of living the gospel that we see as life-giving and able to speak prophetically to the cultural angst of our time. Thus the title In-tensional. Yes, tensional is a word.[1] It speaks of a dynamic tension. Drawn from the Latin word *intênsiõ*, meaning to have strong feeling or tension between two people, objects or ideas, In-tensional describes a tension in which there is strain, stretch and tautness between two people or ideas or objects. We intend naming, creating, and encouraging exactly this tension between two important parts of the Christian church.

In that sense we are attempting something we don't believe has been done before. We want to host a conversation between two sets of people who would not normally read the same book. That is centre-church leaders and edgy missional pioneers. This is not an easy task; we know that what will inspire the edge – people like Justin – will terrify the centre. Equally, what seems like wisdom to centre-church leaders – people like Alan – won't get the radical Jesus followers past the first page. We envisage a conversation between a theologically trained pastor who is comfortable with elders' meetings, sermons, PowerPoint, and pastoral work, and a volunteer pioneer leader who is passionately developing neighbourhood relationships, advocating, protesting and working towards much needed societal change.

It won't be easy to keep both groups reading and engaged with our findings but we are utterly convinced that God's renewal cannot come without this conversation. We are asking you, even daring you, to stick with us and discover more about yourself and what you have to offer the church in the reshaping of its future. But we also need you to listen to 'the other' and see what you can learn from them and how, together, we can move forward in a constructive re-shaping and re-founding of the church in the west.

We want to introduce you to this in-tensional conversation, pointing you to the in-tensional dynamic necessary for our churches to reshape for the needs of our time. We know there will be strong feelings, opposing energies and vigorous critiques. We need to hold these tensions together and see what comes from an in-tensional dialogue that encourages you to foster in-tensional conversations and relationships where you live and work.

We invite you into this critical, in-tensional conversation between the edge and centre of church life, knowing this dynamic will always be uncomfortable, often stretching, and at times contradictory. There will be conflict. This relationship is intense because so much depends on it. We are pushing for a conversation that identifies and normalises the necessary tension between the established centre of church life and its edge because we think the future of the church in the west depends on it.

We believe we have something important to say. Born from our 60-plus years of combined Christian leadership experience – as full of mistakes, failures, and scars as it is of fruitful growth and hope – we can see fresh life coming in ordinary churches across post-secular New Zealand.

We are white male church leaders speaking into a context that is wary of voices like ours, and expect that critiques will come in response to this book because of our ethnicity, gender and social privilege. We welcome critiques because they will further enhance the conversation begun here. We hope to hear alternate voices arise, bringing richer conversations which foster more robust communities of faith.

Reassuringly, while our contemporary context brings unique and immense challenges, God's renewal work has a traceable pattern. Throughout history, when things got desperate, God turned up with a new invitation. If we ever needed a miraculous and transforming God turning up, then it is right now. As we face multiple global crises and a dwindling church, we need to hear a fresh invitation of God's Spirit. We wrote as the COVID-19 pandemic was raging through the world, with an economic crisis surfacing in the pandemic's wake. Now an even greater global crisis – climate change – is bearing down. Covid was a disruptive event, accelerating existing societal trends. As the pandemic died down, some talked of getting back to 'normal' but we all knew there was no return. What lay ahead was a 'new normal'. Now, after the pandemic, we can be certain life and church will look distinctly different.

Alan was living in the city of Christchurch in 2011, when a series of devastating earthquakes hit, destroying the central business district and large areas of the wider city. These earthquakes were a disruptive event propelling trends of church decline and bringing forward necessary decisions in many churches. Small congregations had to make tough choices – did a congregation of 40 to 70 people need or justify the cost of a church rebuild? Would they choose or be forced to combine with a nearby church?

It is true that immediately after the earthquakes some people turned to the church, became Christians, and others returned and became more involved in their church community. However, after this initial response, the trend was towards less frequent attendance, reduced commitment, and many leaving the church. As some moved from their pre-earthquake church to new, independent, trendy alternatives, many more quietly slipped out of regular church engagement altogether.

Today we not only face the aftermath of a global epidemic, another global financial crunch and climate change, there are also deep new cultural disruptions shaped through identity politics and culture wars, expressed, for example, in Black Lives Matter, #MeToo, and the rise of LGBTQI movements. The church's response to such movements is often polarising and includes those who rush to shut discussion down and a conservative deafness to any voice but their own.

At the same time, we in the western world face an unprecedented mental health crisis expressed in rises of anxiety, depression, medication rates and endemic loneliness that further weaken already fragmented communities. In the face of these physical, cultural, and mental health crises we are deeply aware we are standing in a unique moment in history. One from which we believe God is calling us to lead with courage, faithfulness and hope.

Thankfully, God is as gracious as God is powerful and we have a reasonable hope. We can take heart that the church has been through crises before, and these have brought significant change and opened new opportunities. God's invitation at such points in history is demanding. Alan remembers disaster experts predicting that following the Christchurch earthquakes most civil and church leaders would leave their positions, relocate, burn out or give up over the next ten years. The few that survived would be significantly scarred and depleted. Looking back, those experts were right. Today we are entering a new cultural terrain that far exceeds the demands of a series of localised earthquakes. A new cultural moment which calls for courageous, dedicated and wise leadership.

We can only respond to this call of God with the help of His Spirit. So, we say: don't despair God is at work. Equally, don't miss what is required in the face of this challenging crucible of change. This era of church life will cost us everything we have: the best from our innovators on the edge, trying new things but perhaps drifting from the rest of the church body; and the best of our centre-church people working tirelessly, yet likely resistant to the new things God is doing. This challenge requires the whole body of Christ to function at its best and we need each other as much as we need God right now.

We have many churches with strong, established, balanced structures and services and we have para-church groups: energetic pioneering-initiatives and edge mission communities with radical ideas, a counter-cultural approach and innovative community connections. We lack language and means to bring these two together in mutually beneficial ways for the reshaping of the church.

We will talk a lot about centre-church and edge-church because we propose a critical conversation between these two equally essential components of 'church'.[2] They bring different strengths, roles and experience and have different rhythms of life and mission; but they are both worshipping communities of faith centred on Jesus, nourished through scripture and active in God's mission to their communities.

While the word 'church' carries multiple meanings, when we talk of centre-church we mean the established, organised community of people who gather regularly for worship in a particular place. The centre-church generally has regular institutionalised practices and is aligned to a bigger body, a denomination, or is responsible to a structural entity like a group of trustees in the case of an independent church. Edge-church is often seen as radical or fringe and can form as the result of dissatisfaction with centre-church. Edge-church tends to form in smaller groupings with a focussed, whole-of-life commitment to a cause or specific cultural angst. They are characterised by prophetic voices and a sense of call to the marginalised.

We are not promoting one style of church over the other. We are not saying one is the answer for the future. Quite the opposite; we are claiming that both centre and edge are church. Both are essential to the future of the church in the west. The table below lists some names we will use to distinguish the centre and edge.

Centre	Edge
Centre-church	Edge-dwellers
Congregation	Community
Centre-leaders	Edge-leaders
Focused more on Pastors and Teachers	Focused more on Prophetic and Apostolic leaders

Before continuing, we need to name a widely accepted way of thinking about edge and centre within churches, mission agencies and theological colleges, which is based on Ralph Winter's 1973 paper on the dichotomy of modalities and sodalities.[3] While the Catholic church and social historians had identified this dynamic at work for centuries it was Ralph Winter who introduced the terms modalities and sodalities, into protestant mission language and understandings. In his dichotomy modalities reflect the established church and sodalities the more missional groupings.[4] Modality and sodality describe different roles, energies and focuses, but both are integral parts of the church. We have called these centre-church (modality like) and edge-church (sodality like). From our perspective, both are part of, and necessary to, the church. The sad demise of the church in the west has been enhanced by the separation of the modality and sodality energies when the two become disconnected from each other.[5] For example, when what are often called 'para-church groups' (sodality) become separated for long periods from the wider church (modality).

We believe centre-church and edge-church need each other, and neither holds the hope of the future by themselves. They need to engage in this in-tensional conversation in order to be the church and follow God's calling.

Our stories of centre and edge

Justin, it's fair to say, is naturally an edge-dweller. Most comfortable without shoes, haircuts or new clothes, he finds church services and vestry meetings horrendously boring. Growing up in a working-class neighbourhood he loved being a youth worker. He spent a decade working with kids outside the church, created a home for kids without one and lived life in the dirtier end of the city, making friends and being family with homeless guys and sex workers.

Leaving city life, Justin and his wife Jenny spent the next decade transforming an old campsite into a refuge for those needing a rural retreat, or those trying to make it fresh from prison or a mental health crisis. Justin and Jenny tried to call the church outwards by inspiring them to put a gospel theology into action in the world. The resulting Urban Vision community is their primary tribe of belonging and they couldn't survive and minister without them. This community has a passion for justice, a highly committed, living faith in Jesus and a deep corporate belonging as they live together in small teams of believers.

These days Urban Vision people live in ten teams, typically in neighbourhoods where people find themselves on the margins of society. They try to respond as good neighbours, rather than professionals or service providers, sharing life and working for transformation at personal and communal levels.

Ten years ago, in some wacky combination of God's prophetic humour and creativity, coupled with the courage of the Anglican church, Justin was called to lead the Anglican diocese as the Bishop of Wellington. The diocese was aware of its rapid decline in numbers, its growing distance from the surrounding culture and a dread that, without something fresh and new, it was in big trouble. They knew they had plenty to offer the world and a deep faith that God was not finished with them yet. So, they asked Jenny and Justin to come and live among them, bringing their passion for the neighbourhood, their concern for the planet and their lifestyle of community building and pioneer mission.

Justin had never done paid work for the church before and it has been a big transition adjusting to the traditions and structures of a diocese and getting his heart around a culture that is very different to his roots. In this new context, he has sought to hear God's invitation to the church in this rapidly changing culture. His journey has taken him from residing happily on the edge of the church to needing to discover the gifts of the church's very centre.

Alan has spent 35 years smack in the centre of Baptist church life: as centre-church as it gets. Growing up in a middle-class family, he attended an evangelical church that was powerfully influenced by the charismatic movement of the late 1970's. Later he moved from being an Air Force officer to train as a pastor in a large Baptist church in Christchurch, New Zealand; a shift downward in pay, social respect, role and opportunities and a step up in work hours, study and people's expectations. He loved this dynamic, innovative and missionally focussed church and enjoyed preaching and teaching, studying theology and sociology, and developing the next generation of church leaders.

Arriving at Central Baptist in Wellington, in time Alan became the senior pastor in a church committed to social justice and innovative mission. In this mix were the founders of Stillwaters, a place for the city's street community. Stillwaters offered weekday lunches and a social drop-in space on Friday nights. The church's Stillwaters ministry later partnered with Urban Vision, led by Justin and Jenny Duckworth. The Duckworth family had moved into Stillwaters' community house in the inner city, along with many of their friends. It was a very tight fit. This was not an easy relationship. The Central Baptist ministry team liked to keep set hours, tidy spaces and workable rosters. The Urban Vision crew tended to be untidy, unpredictable, operated an open-door policy and were critical of Sunday church! But the church leadership were up for the challenge of hosting this diversity and saw the potential gifts that both the edge and the centre had to offer.

After ten years in Wellington, Alan was called to be senior pastor in the Christchurch church where he'd trained: a complex church with many ministries and a strong global focus. With the associated trusts, church staff, and global teams there were hundreds of employees and many more who called the church home. Two years later when the earthquakes struck, leading a large, diverse church became very stretching. Two things became clear: firstly, the western church, with its present form and focus, was in serious decline and losing engagement with people and culture; secondly, two small, local intentional communities (similar to the Urban Vision crew), who had been part of the church for some time, were offering a new, energising way of being.

One of these intentional communities had all recently moved into a poor city neighbourhood, cramming into several small houses and engaging with their neighbours by sharing everything from time and meals to gardens and spare rooms. Houses in this neighbourhood were cheap, so the group pooled their savings to buy an old petrol station and create a café. Twelve years on it employs dozens of people including locals from their neighbourhood. Eighty percent of the profits from the café and associated businesses – laundromat, fairtrade coffee roastery and gift shop – are donated to local community development initiatives, and to business and community work in Kolkata, India.

Alan found himself pastoring two groups within this one church: the first group were critical of 'the church', demanding more engagement with the poor, with neighbourhood projects, and social issues; the other was the stable congregation who believed in community-focused ministries without the need for intentional personal community living. Taking up the missional challenge presented to them, Alan, and wife Sandra, committed to greater neighbourhood engagement and local community building.

Fast forward 10 years and the church had several groups living intentionally in their respective neighbourhoods. These local groups worked together, prayed for and offered hospitality and friendship within their respective neighbourhoods. The church leadership encouraged these local communities to share their passion and expertise for intentional, missional, community-based life with the wider church. It created a fascinating learning tension. Recently Alan started a new role leading the Baptist Churches of New Zealand's global work, which is giving him a view into denominational structures, established churches and new missional endeavours on the global scene. His journey in Christian leadership has taken him from the centre of church life and leadership to finding the necessary gifts for church renewal on the prophetic edge.

Hosting the courageous conversation that might reshape the church

We have both observed, studied and experienced the repeated tensions that characterise life between the edge and centre of the church. We have heard the critiques of centre-church leaders and edge-innovators. Sadly, we have watched centre-church and edge-church pull apart at times, missing their desperate need for each other. We have both lived inside this relationship with all its tension, heartbreak, and frustration, alongside the life, energy and joy it can bring. We have seen the hopeful creativity and renewing power possible through edge and centre working together and learning from each other.

In chapter 1, we will outline the reality of the global crisis facing our generation, as well as the state of our western church. It's a challenging reality as we summarise the state of an insipid church, unfit for the task of bringing sharp insight and life-giving alternatives in our world. Edge-dwellers will say 'I told you so' as we briefly outline these stark realities. Centre-church leaders will no doubt feel defensive, or despair at the starkly depressing state of the church in the west.

In chapter 2, we will outline the prophetic calling on the church to offer a feasible alternative and a hopeful, exciting future. We will point out that the charisms and callings necessary for our current generation can be most sharply seen lived out in fragile missional groups who find themselves on the edge of church life.

Then we'll get practical with models of how this relationship works at its healthiest. We will compare a healthy relationship tension with times when the intensity blows out and becomes destructive. For three decades we have lived in this relationship, experiencing the best and worst of it, in several different churches and cities. We know this territory well.

If you are a centre-church reader, be reassured that we are not asking you to move to an undesirable neighbourhood or quit work to live in communal flats with ex-prisoners and psychiatric patients. We are asking centre-church leaders to listen to edge-pioneers and their prophetic communities to inspire, inform and influence your life and priorities and those of your churches.

If you are part of an intentional mission endeavour, we are not asking you to be at a Sunday service every week, to join the vestry or sing on stage. However, you will need to recognise the enduring and significant role of the established church and its leaders and what they bring to the reshaping of the church for tomorrow. You can't do it without them.

Next, we will point out how the church has been reformed and found new life through the centuries. Hopefully this will inspire you to stick with us as we see the same themes unfolding again in our own contexts. We will point to moments in church history where, in seasons of church decline and societal irrelevance, God called and raised up small prophetic groups. These groups were accepted and supported by the established church, and were living a particular gospel charism, needed for that time. A charism that eventually called the church on to greater faithfulness and fruitfulness.

If we can keep you reading, there are things edge-dwellers will need to know about centre-church leaders, and vice-versa. Equally, there are things for centre-church leaders to reflect on together and things groups of edge-dwellers need to reflect on and re-orient around.

In chapter 4 we will tell the imaginary story of Mia, a young radical who has become a follower of Jesus and has a heart for people like her who are searching for truth and hope but dismiss the church as irrelevant to them. Having introduced you to Mia we outline two divergent paths she could travel depending on the advice, support and encouragement she receives from key leaders around her.

Chapter 5 describes what edge and centre respectively can bring to an in-tensional relationship and the typical life cycle of edge communities. If you want to jump to the heart of this book, read the summary of chapter 5 and focus on chapters 6 to 8, describing the three stages of the edge-community life cycle: radical to sustainable to influential. Finally, in chapter 9, we bring the whole argument together and ask: could God be at work through centre and edge bringing a reshaping and reinvigorating of His church for a new cultural context?

Summary

❖ Justin speaks the language of the edge and knows well their heart and function but has learnt to converse in the language of centre-church and to appreciate the gifts they offer. Alan has learnt to understand the edge but remains fluent in centre-church life and leadership and understands the best and worst of it. We are all called differently, and we respect God's different callings on our lives. We ask you to allow each other's gifts and insights to speak into your reality and to foster in-tensional relationships across centre and edge church.

❖ While it's repetitive to constantly use the terms 'edge' and 'centre', it encapsulates a vital point. Without the 'edge' western churches will continue to die; their buildings will increasingly become cafés and boutique furniture shops and their communities will miss out on the passionate renewal God wants to bring to the western church. Worse still, we will be complicit in the ongoing destruction of the world through continuing to mirror the values of our time. Values which at their core are idolatrous to God and destroy people and planet. Without the centre, the edge, in their fragility, will not sustain themselves for the long haul. They are in constant danger of bitterness or pride undermining them. Without belonging deeply to the wider body of the church these edge groups will remain small and peripheral, their prophetic voice lost or muted.

❖ We argue that without this conversation between edge and centre the western church will spiral further down the track of irrelevance, failing to grasp contemporary culture, unable to align with God's calling to this generation. We believe our union is necessary for the re-shaping, re-vitalising and re-founding of the church in the west. Only centre and edge united can speak to the deepest angst and questions of our time.

❖ We can't keep isolating the edge from the centre of the church. We believe in unity and working in harmony and other important biblical values, but this is also about the future shape and life of the church. Your church and your community desperately need the fruit of this vital conversation. Through this book we want to give you working models of how these differently gifted groups of the church can and must work together.

Chapter 1 — Facing our Reality

We are screwed. Seriously. Everywhere we look there are fundamental crises, threats and systems out of control. Twenty years ago, Alan taught Sociology when one of the leading theorists of the time, Anthony Giddens, described western society as a juggernaut. It is a powerful image. The word juggernaut comes from a Hindu practice in which an extremely heavy vehicle with large wheels is dragged through a city. People throw themselves under the wheels and are crushed to death by the sheer weight of the vehicle. This image hints at the horror the juggernaut induced. In sociology a juggernaut is a powerful, completely unsteerable engine that is running riot with extreme consequences.

While back then the image sparked great theoretical debate, today it often feels like we are the passengers on the juggernaut, screaming headlong towards multiple global crises with no driver and only dubious steering capacity even if someone could, or would, reach for the controls. For many in the west, riding first-class on the juggernaut is quite pleasant, certainly compared to those in western poverty or majority world despair. Nevertheless, we are all passengers on this vehicle that's heading to any number of disastrous and catastrophic ends: international terror threats, community violence, refugee crises, global climate change, recurring pandemics, stock and currency market threats, housing, water and health care shortages, increasing levels of mental unhealth, prescribed and illegal drug dependence, endemic crime, imprisonment and recidivism cycles, family dysfunction and breakdown. The list just goes on.

Any sober and serious assessment of modern life and our global future must acknowledge the unprecedented disparities and imminent disastrous outcomes surrounding us. On a macro, societal level these are huge. On a personal, micro level we most often ignore them, as we figuratively try to close the curtains on the juggernaut windows and eat, drink and make merry. For a moment we want to look further at both these macro and micro perspectives.

Sociologists use many big words to try and name what is changing – terms like post-modernity, globalisation, tribalism, post-

Christendom, endemic economic disparity, religious pluralism, and a crisis of democracy. Whatever the concepts, getting a handle on the current shifts and drivers is at best slippery and foggy. What is clear – and universally recognized – is that this change is fundamental, significant and unrelenting in its pace. The significant changes can be summarised under seven – by no means exhaustive – headings.

1. **A Crisis of Meaning**. Under the influence of post-modernity (some would say post-post-modernity) the western world is increasingly characterised by people's distrust of big, meaningful stories, what sociologists call meta-narratives. Whether these are historic meta-narratives, or new ones, whether religious, political, emancipatory or ideological, we see a growing distrust of such big stories. With this comes a growing distrust of experts and authorities, truth claims and 'so called' facts. In the wake of agreed stories of meaning, instead people are turning to personal stories of identity and uniqueness.

2. **A Crisis of Hope**. With the loss of plausible meta-narratives that have anchored societies through all known history comes a loss of belief in progress and a lack of confidence in the future bringing a better world. Ecologically, economically, religiously, scientifically, philosophically, even in terms of trust in democratic and legal systems there is growing cynicism and a vacuum of hope.

3. **A Crisis of Belonging**. With the demands for easily movable labour through the rise of capitalism, core institutions of belonging – extended families, workplaces, unions, political parties and social organisations – have broken down. The result is a crisis of belonging. Increasingly people feel alone, as if relationships, even family relationships, are temporary and they have no deep sense of identity or belonging.

4. **A Crisis of Debt**. A fundamental move in the underlying driver of our economic systems has been the move from a production and savings driven economy to a consumption and debt driven economy. Increasingly we live in a 'buy now, pay later world' which, with student loans, rampant house prices and increasing personal expectations for commodity ownership and personal experiences, has introduced a growing debt crisis.

The assessments of personal and government debt in western countries are of eye-watering proportions.

5. **A Crisis of Reality**. With the explosion of communication technology and social media, the previous fixed certainties of time and space have increasingly dissolved. This leads to either a dislocation between our on-line and off-line worlds or, more scarily, a crisis in what is real in our lives.

6. **Crisis of Participation.** A growing distrust and disbelief in democratic and government systems, fuelled by a growing belief that those in charge of large companies, multinational corporations and governments are acting for their own gain rather than the good of society, has bred a reluctance to participate. The critic and the un-engaged far outnumber the committed participants of the essential systems of our society, including democracy, civil society, religion or movements of social reform.

7. **Crisis of Identity**. Being dislodged from stable senses of place, family, meta-narratives and community of belonging, and being exposed to exponential volumes of information and mediated, disembodied communications have cumulatively enhanced many people's identity crisis.

How society reached this point is the focus of many academics' lives, fills numerous books and, to varying degrees, is information readers have heard before. Our focus here is simply to outline this societal crisis as a foundation to a fuller discussion of renewal in the church.

One of the core outcomes of these societal crises has been the rise of individualism. Individualism encourages an unhealthily inflated ego and can be seen as a self-centred aggrandisement or a personal and spiritual grandiosity. Robert Moore depicts this personal grandiosity rampant in our culture of individualism as an internal dragon.[6] This dragon of individualism that lurks to varying degrees in us all is shown in a dominant and unchecked focus on what I want – my agenda, my desires, my comfort, etc. Individualism has become unrivalled as the post-modern idol. The table below summarises individualism's main components:

Individualism – "Me, myself, I"	
Consumerism	*I get what I want whenever I want it*
Careerism	*I put my career first*
Commutism	*I travel, live and relate where I want when I want*
Compartmentalism	*I live my life in separate pieces to protect myself*

Of course, individual freedom is precious but that is quite different to our cultural capitulation to individualism. In contemporary culture our individual freedom goes unchecked by a greater cause, a prior social responsibility, or a faith that keeps our focus beyond ourselves. Individual choice has been elevated to the point where it undermines both personal responsibility and our collective good. This untamed dragon within has divided and isolated us.

In the wake of global juggernauts and the internal dragon of personal individualism we are left to find our own way. This overwhelming aloneness in the wake of enormous global threats has led to many personal stresses and varied breakdowns. However, it has also led to an increasing interest in spirituality, and a growing desire for deep community and counter-cultural forms of living that tackle global and personal threats with hopeful responsibility.

The western church is often the last place those seeking spirituality, hopeful community and responsible living look. While society has been overtaken (Giddens' juggernaut) and individuals swamped (Moore's internal dragon) the church in the west has been declining and ageing and is increasingly irrelevant. This is at best ironic and at worst a catastrophe. When our culture most needs the church to provide a hopeful, purposeful and world-affirming way of life, the church flounders and declines and is effectively mute on today's issues.

Alan's Ph.D. research and his subsequent books focused on the faith of people outside the church. From research like this and 30 years of personal experience, we are convinced that while there is unprecedented growth of the Christian faith and church in Africa, Asia and Latin America, there is also a consistent and increasing decline in the churches of western countries. It began in northern Europe in countries like Denmark and in the southern antipodes in countries like New Zealand, and over recent decades has spread to encompass all Western Europe, North America, South Africa and Australia. The trajectory of decline within the church in these countries is both alarming and undeniable. Many research projects, theses and books give statistics and personal narratives of this widespread and accelerating church decline and it is not our intent to focus on that here.

In recent years the mega-church meltdowns have brought media attention to massive systemic failures in what had been seen as a new church form that was growing and bringing hope for the church in the west. Today mega-churches are toppling. Of course, we are all aware of churches that are growing, and their success seems to offer a pattern for others to follow. However, these hopeful glimpses are only making a miniscule impact on the overall trend and are at times misleading. The growth of these churches is invariably built on transfer growth from other churches, effectively shifting the already convinced from one church to another, more attractive one.

There are exceptions, but typically one church's growth comes as people leave smaller, often more traditional churches and move to the new, independent, 'hip' alternative. Let's remember, most independent churches draw young people and families with teenagers from other churches. These transfers mask any growth due to people coming to faith for the first time, and changing churches does little for the deepening discipleship of the movers. Research, though scant, suggests the big 'hip' churches have around the same percentage rate of converts as smaller churches.

Often fast-growing churches also have wide open back doors, and many people leave as easily as they came. At least in the New Zealand context, fast-growing charismatic and independent Pentecostal churches are typically one generational. Their defining characteristic tends to be a charismatic and gifted leader who is shown to be irreplaceable by the subsequent decline in attendance once they hand the reins to a second generation of leadership. When we lift our focus above that of individual churches, we see this rise and fall is doing little to halt the wider, unrelenting trend of church decline.

Some will want to push back on this trajectory of decline by pointing to the growth of churches among immigrant communities in the west. Driven by immigration, strong cultural cohesion and family motivation to retain their practices of worship, these churches are growing. They provide a significant place of belonging in a new culture. This immigration-driven growth boosts baptism and evangelism numbers, but these growing churches mask the overall rates of decline. Research into ethnic churches show they don't, in fact, have stronger multi-generational commitments than western Christians. That is, the children and grandchildren of immigrants, influenced more by western culture than their traditional culture, still leave their parents' and grandparents' churches in high numbers.

Age is another factor. As Justin says of the Anglican church in New Zealand, we are not only declining but also rapidly ageing. Taken together, these declining and ageing demographics mean if the tipping point into devastating decline has not yet been reached, it's close.

An even more significant difficulty for the church is our wider society's perception of the Christian faith, and the Christian church, as judgmental, boring, intolerant and irrelevant to contemporary concerns and global crises.

However, in wider western society, there is a growing hunger and search for a purposeful spirituality: a desire to talk and explore openly with others around deep issues of faith. This is coupled with an admiration and respect for those who live faith-filled counter-cultural lives which address specific issues of our time. We (Justin and Alan) both experience this spiritual hunger and openness in the people we meet – and their dismissal of the church as irrelevant to their search.

"This is why I am so glad to be a Bishop in the Anglican church in New Zealand now", says Justin. "The challenges we face as New Zealand Anglicans are facing all western churches. So, as we 'grasp the nettle' others can learn from our mistakes and be encouraged to join us as we look harsh realities in the face and find new ways forward. We need to acknowledge the pain and attempt to adjust to the context we find ourselves in while being faithful to God and our inherited faith. Then we will be wrestling with issues that are crucially important not just to the Wellington Anglican diocese, or the New Zealand church, but the whole Western church. We believe that, as the old saying goes, '*Insanity is doing the same thing over and over again but expecting different results*'. In this case, it means if we don't change, we risk going quietly into the night. The good news is that there is a powerful alternative."

Before starting to imagine God's alternative, we are aware that some churches are growing, and the leaders of these churches probably won't see any point in this book. For them the answer is clear: if church leaders want to see growth, they need to do as we do. That response makes sense, and we would say 'go for it', if it is working and you have found a niche of growth in the out-going cultural tide. When the tide is going out some boats do find deeper pools and stay afloat but it won't happen for everyone. So, if you're not a charismatic leader fishing in a niche pool let's reimagine together where God may be speaking into our cultural context in fresh ways.

If we can reimagine church for this generation then the impact will be far reaching. We believe this is the longing of God and through reading church history we see God's faithful work at successive similar points. For us this opens a great opportunity to faithfully serve our God in our contexts.

First, we need to address two common responses among church leaders. We have spoken with many leaders in New Zealand, Europe, North America and Australia about the realities of church decline and the church's lack of alignment with society's longings. Their response to these stark realities is often to retreat to one of two theological positions, both of which we find problematic.

The first is an acceptance of the statistics of decline and comes in two guises. There is sometimes a wistful reply that as the church loses nominal believers, a kind of purifying happens within the church. This implies the decline is a necessary cleansing and therefore positive. This response tends to conclude by saying we will end up with the highly committed, remnant church who will remain steadfast after the nominals have been weeded out. This weeding out is all part of the great plan that sets the stage for a coming revival. This is not true. Many of those staying in the church are not highly committed to a steadfast hope of future revival, but people of low religious commitment or rapidly advancing age.

The second guise is church leaders who accept the reality of church decline and think we just need to dutifully bear the burden of a Church heading towards extinction. All that church leaders are asked to do is faithfully lead in ways that amount to little more than palliative care; as if the future is totally up to God, and we must simply watch God's purposes unfold. While we absolutely agree that the future is up to God, we also see God at work bringing renewing life and direction. We need to recognize this life and direction, and work with God in order to foster and support it being brought into our churches and communities. The sad reality is that many churches miss a new move of God and don't change. Not because God doesn't want them to change but because the leaders and community of the church don't play their part.

Church history repeatedly presents a troubled church heading towards disaster and yet somehow God, faithful to his covenant with his people, has renewed the church over and over. God most often worked through prophetically entrepreneurial leaders who he raised up because they were available and trusted him to be at work – even in a dying church – to bring new life. Ultimately, we believe in Jesus' resurrection. Therefore, we believe that we are a resurrection people. God's church really does belong to God, and we are active participants in its renewal.

This is where the second response of many Church leaders comes to the surface. They appear to believe only other churches are declining. Their own church will be fine; God will renew it without fundamental change. No work to be done here! This is not the historical reality that we have come to understand. Yes, God is always renewing the church through bringing new perspectives on biblical truths, forms and focuses. However, history shows us that particular expressions of church have become extinct many times before when they do not align to what God is doing.

We believe that God seeks to renew the church and it is our choice whether to be part of this future. It is a choice that many generations have had to make in the past. Some have listened and embarked on an adventurous journey into the unknown, following their sense of God's guidance. Others have stuck to the seeming safety of the known. As leaders of churches in the western world, we find ourselves at these cross-roads again. This is the time to listen to the voice and signs of the Spirit and take courage as we turn away from the traps of fatalism or triumphalism. It is time to embrace the spiritual orientation of a faithful people in pilgrimage with God's renewing Spirit.

To move beyond these two common responses we need to look at the state of the church in the west. Our congregations are ageing, our numbers are decreasing, and we are missing the deep angst, questions and concerns of our time. The church in the west has been compromised by a consumerism that has made church simply another consumer choice.

Having some level of church engagement is seen as a commodity chosen according to personal taste, rather than a community of people committed to God and each other through thick and thin. The typical experience of people in church communities is not a deep and costly commitment to a faith-community in which our faith is honed through hard times. It is not an experience in which the depth of our commitment grows deeper through conflict, honesty, forgiveness, shared cost, deep prayer and loyalty. It is not an experience of truly living the fruits of the Spirit in relationship together.

There is little sign that we are God's people living out the gospel of fellowship and faithfulness, enduring love and commitment to each other. On the contrary, we typically move churches as we move supermarkets: based on the best deals for us. Equally, church leaders have learnt much from the school of consumerism, marketing their churches to people's tastes, preaching what people want to hear and asking less and less of their congregations beyond attendance and tithes. Is this the Kingdom of God?

We have become idolatrous, focussing our lives on money, careers, cardboard cut-out nuclear families, and the western dream of health, wealth and happiness, without contrary teaching from the church and a willingness to name these as sites of sin in our lives. We have taken on the 'gods' of our time and the church is no longer the place to grapple with how we dethrone and disempower these idols in our lives. Justin tells the story of meeting a man at a church who said he and his fellow congregants only had an hour and a half a week to be church together. When Justin asked why, the man replied, "Well we live in relatively expensive homes that mean sustaining substantial mortgages". That was a given at their church. The man explained, "This means we have demanding jobs." Another given. "Our homes are havens for our families". Another given. Children's after-school activities, sports and friendships were another given.

There were more taken-for-granted and unchallenged life expectations carried by this man: necessary holidays (often in other countries), newish cars and recreational activities like biking, sailing and weekends at the holiday home. Put it all together and the 'givens' of this man's lifestyle mean he and people like him have very little time left over for church. Sadly, when he came to church these expectations and lifestyle choices were not discussed, let alone challenged.

Challenging this kind of accepted lifestyle would be suicide for a pastor and necessitate an uncomfortable discussion. We are aware of sounding judgemental in an age where being judgemental is the worst of sins. We can't ask people to repent without naming the idol they have chosen to worship. We begin where any mental health counsellor would begin, by naming reality so that the choice for health and the opportunity to change can be clearly seen. Where do we hear the prayers of reformers like Ignatius, whose cry for a genuine encounter with Christ was based on a desire that "we ought not to seek health rather than sickness, wealth rather than poverty, honour rather than dishonour, a long life rather than a short one..." rather we ought to desire only that which we were created for "to praise, reverence and serve God our Lord"?[7] We don't hear this message being so starkly preached and discussed in today's growing churches because doing so would offend the consumer mindsets and accepted 'givens' of our time.

An examination of our fitness in faith, our strength in prayer, our commitment to studying scripture, our hospitality habits, our love for our neighbours and our understanding of theology often exposes us as unpractised, undisciplined and poorly prepared for service. In contrast, when we have visited churches in persecuted countries, and Christians in the desperately poor regions of the world, we have observed quite different expressions of faith, service and what it means to take up one's cross. Too often our churches in the west are simply flabby when it comes to the practices of discipleship and the choice to live radically counter-cultural lives following the one who carried his own difficult cross.

Finally, our churches are so often best described as insipid. They are not connected to the deep lows of people's pain, depression, fear and darkness, nor the laughter, energy and fullness of human love and life that would make them radically attractive places.

People just have better things to do with their time than engage with what they see of church today.

We are highly critical of the church because we believe in the church and have great hope for what it can be. We critique what the church has become from a position of love and commitment. We believe God is reforming the church in the west. However, we also believe that God does this quietly and from the edges and we could very easily miss what God is doing and where God is doing it.

Summary

❖ In this chapter, we have argued that the church in New Zealand – and by extension the church in the western world today – is significantly out of alignment with the needs and spiritual longings of their own communities. While many people outside the church have deep spiritual longings, real faith questions and a quest for purpose and meaning in their lives, they are not looking to the church to meet these desires. For many the church does not represent a safe or welcoming place to satisfy these hungers.

❖ There is also a second layer of concern. From our experience we perceive the western church to be significantly out of alignment with God: idolatrous, compromised, flabby and insipid. Our faith has gone cold. We are known more often for our hypocrisy than our wholehearted holiness.

❖ These are big claims, and you may wish to close the book at this point. But we believe our perspective is justified. More importantly these critiques, and others, need to be acknowledged and discussed. We desperately need to enter this conversation.

Chapter 2 — Process of Renewal

Having clarified the grim realities of the western church and culture, and stated our belief that God is nevertheless working to renew our churches, how do we realign ourselves? How do we become a transformative church in tune with cultural needs and gospel imperatives? How can the church actively speak to deep cultural angst and people's pain with the good news of the gospel?

Many church leaders will agree that we need something fresh, passionate and strong enough to turn the tide of our dwindling reality. We long for it deeply, yet if our current leaders and church leadership could manage this then wouldn't they have done it by now? To centre-church leaders, pastors and ministers leading congregations, denominational and mission group leaders and those in church governance and leadership roles, we want to say: the way forward is not to try harder or add something new to what you're already doing. We hope that relieves you of a sense of burden. However, you do have a crucial role to play.

Consider the five-fold ministry described in Ephesians, and how that plays out in our churches. Ephesians describes church leadership made up of apostles, pastors, teachers, evangelists and prophets. Our established churches, that we are calling centre-church, favour and tend to train and reproduce leaders in pastoral and teaching skills and roles. Some church settings also incorporate a significant place for evangelists, especially those who also have strong pastoral or teaching giftings. But centre-church structures don't encourage, train and empower prophets and apostles into leadership in anything like the necessary numbers.

Alan fits the stereotypical teacher-pastor leader. Justin, on the other hand, is an apostolic leader. While Alan enjoyed theological training, Justin found it unbearable. Both love reading and thinking and have their share of degrees but while Alan is at home in the classroom and the pulpit, Justin gravitated to a far more active learning. This included risky experimentation in lived theology, the critique of our present church realities and critical engagement with what God is calling us into. Justin loved walking with mentors who were living costly mission lifestyles, visiting them overseas to learn by watching their lives and living in their communities. We are both naturally, and in terms of focus, experience and training, different types of leaders who have primarily led in different contexts.

From our experience and conversations together, we believe that a large part of the church transforming process begins when God raises up prophetic and apostolic groups on the edge of the church. These people call us back to a new faithfulness and fruitfulness in terms of engagement with the needs and pains of the wider community. Prophetic and apostolic leaders carry the gifts and skills needed to find us new paths forward; their prophetic and apostolic charisms create faith ventures and communities that challenge us where we have become tired and idolatrous.

Yet these leaders are not often given space to lead in today's churches. More typically they are disillusioned, their giftings not fully accepted, or they are way out on the edge, beyond connection with a local church and the recognition of centre-church leaders. Some edge-dwellers choose to be disconnected from centre-church because of prior experiences and may feel that on the edge they are not drained by the aspects of centre-church life they have struggled with. We understand that feeling but we, the centre-church, need their interaction and engagement to help us transform!

To do this we need centre-church leaders – that is the pastor/ teacher types in our established churches – to reach out to and listen to the edge dwelling prophetic and apostolic leaders. Centre-church leaders need to form significant relationships with them, and to understand that listening to their concerns will require holding a necessary tension.

We, the centre-church leaders, need to learn how to relate to these edge-leaders and their experimental faith ventures and communities, and to allow them to be themselves in our churches. Let's invite them to be the 'inside-edge' of our churches. Being on the 'inside-edge' means they are outside the regular patterns and programmes of the church but are connected, known and in relationship with the centre-church leaders and the church community more broadly. It's a real relationship that says there is a necessary place and role for these leaders and their communities alongside centre-church leaders and alongside centre-church life and structures. That is alongside, but not demandingly engaged with centre church.

It may help to see the group we are calling edge-dwellers through another lens. Twenty-five years ago Alan completed a Ph.D. on the faith journeys of church leavers. In that he described one segment of leavers as wayfinders: the people who find and lead the way. This word is also used by Māori to describe Polynesian navigators who would leave their settled home in search of unknown lands which could provide food, new crops or a place to live. These Polynesian wayfinders are described as those who "go beyond the known, and journey on voyages of discovery to new horizons."[8] They didn't use western means of navigation but drew on other forms of intelligence like reading the swell pattern of the waves, the shape and path of clouds, streaks of phosphorescence on the tip of waves, the flight path of birds and the night sky. For example, the ancient wayfinders might lie on the bottom of their sailing vessel feeling and hearing the wave patterns and discerning the echo of land in the rhythm and vibration of the successive waves they felt through their body.

It is not only Polynesian sailors who were wayfaring and utilising wayfinding skills. These same ways are part of the stories of the Inuit who travelled across vast snow plains, Aboriginal Australians who trekked the deserts and Bedouin nomads who traversed sand dune landscapes. Using this imagery, the edge-dwellers could be likened to wayfinders. They leave the known to explore the unknown. Seeking to find new ways and new treasures. We are convinced that by allowing the prophetic and apostolic edge-dwellers to function more healthily alongside the life of our churches, we will see renewal. These movements call the church to renewal, and they show us how to sense the Kingdom come in the present context of disillusionment and decay.

Biblically the aim is for the church body to have all its members working together healthily and actively. Unintentionally centre-church leaders can alienate and ignore the very leaders and potential new movements that are most needed. Centre-church leaders can prioritise the voice and role of teacher-pastors, allowing them to dominate our churches and prevent any side-line prophetic and apostolic leaders and edge-groups from bringing their gifts. Edge-dwellers can dismiss centre-church and its leaders, failing to engage and letting their criticism undermine relationships with those committed to and leading centre-churches.

This vision in which centre and edge can engage constructively is complicated by the protestant practice of separating new, experimental movements from established churches, either as para-church groups or new churches. (This is an inherently protestant practice. Historical Catholicism has often managed to hold congregations, communities, orders and parishes together as one church, though not without some failures and great tension.) The practice of splitting the new from the established can give the new more freedom and opportunities but without intentional connection it also severs it from the insight, wisdom, resources and reach of the established church and separates the established church from the innovation, energy and learnings of the edge-dwellers.

While centre and edge do occupy distinct roles and functions in the church, and they do have different orientations to each other; they do not need to be separate. Too often, at least in the New Zealand settings that we have observed, centre and edge are isolated, even alienated from each other, so that everyone loses. To quote George Lings "If the tension is held well then, the sodal (edge) acts to renew, and thus to change, the life in the modal (centre). Andrew Walls adds the further scary scenario that God does this not just out of missional creativity but because the existing modal church can be sick and is facing future extinction."[9]

Our understanding of how apostolic and prophetic leaders work best with pastoral and teaching leaders has been lost. Typically, the new is relegated to the margins, beyond the edge, where it must compete against the centre-church for people's time and donations. The possibility of regaining a healthy dynamic is dim, and complicated by the usual battles born of our personal insecurities, fears, pride and ego drives. That has been the same through the centuries, and as we'll show you in the next chapter, there are examples we can follow. It's the pattern of church history. It's the way God has always brought renewal to his people. Before we explore historical renewal movements let's consider the role of prophetic and apostolic movements more deeply.

Edge defined

What are the essential characteristics of the apostolic-prophetic movements, or edge-dwellers? Firstly, they are highly committed groups who hold a white-hot faith. Of course, we should all, as Christ followers, have a highly committed faith. But for these edge-dwelling leaders and their apostolic-prophetic movements, deep radical commitment is what is modelled and expected as the necessary way of life to live into the dreams and callings they follow.

These apostolic-prophetic people will form themselves into covenanted or highly committed communities. They call others to join them in committing to their visions and causes. Belonging to one of these communities costs the individual and they are not easy spaces for people with limited time or energy. Nor are they spaces for the doubting or the dualists who are pursuing both a Christian life and a secular career, following popular societal values or wedded to the recognition of the crowd. This is not the space for those who follow "God and ..." but for those who follow "God only".

These communities tend to live and model a holistic Christian lifestyle and are prepared to pay the price such a lifestyle demands. They commit to deep belonging, genuine vulnerability and open accountability in a shared life of rich faith. To those in centre-church such covenanted communities and committed lifestyles begin to ring alarm bells. People used to centre-church sense that those in the apostolic communities are living unbalanced lives. And they are right. This reality often challenges centre-church people, questioning their norms and highlighting their own choices; and – dare we say it – their own idolatries. Idolatries so normalised in our culture and churches that to live differently seems both wrong and personally threatening.

Lastly and most importantly these apostolic edge communities are missionally focussed, and completely captivated by a particular gospel imperative. The gospel imperative that each group embraces will be different: issues of social justice, concern for the ecological environment, bold new evangelism approaches, local community development, compassion for the poor or a particular marginalised people group are just some examples. Whatever their gospel imperative, they feel a strong calling to respond to an aching need of those they are committed to with white-hot faith and a holistic lifestyle. They have something specific, tangible and compelling to get up for in the morning. It is a passionate calling to see the Kingdom come where it has not yet come.

Apostolic, evangelistic and prophetic gifts and callings are present in established institutional churches too, but in this setting there are not enough of these leaders in influential positions and roles and their gifts are not typically honoured and promoted. They are not able to be as effective in bringing significant gospel focused change. When the apostolic and prophetic leaders gather and form mission endeavours on the edges of our churches, they are more effective at pioneering, planting and reaching new mission fields than the rest of the church will ever be. It is their gift.

The central-church leaders, typically gifted pastorally and as teachers, are not very good at this apostolic and prophetic work. They may be highly committed but this commitment is expressed differently to the counter-cultural ways of the edge-dwellers. The apostolic and prophetic types on the edge often intuitively speak the language of those who are hungry for spirituality but dismissive of the church, and they instinctively resonate with the hungers and longings of our wider culture. They are prepared to start something new which can speak to the needs, hungers and longings they and their friends in the wider culture experience. They will pay the personal price of forming communities in counter-cultural ways which earn them respect and credibility when engaging others.

This is not to say centre-church leaders do not also pay high prices, but that they do so differently. The communities and approaches edge-dwellers form when linked to the centre-church, can bring great life and hope back into our churches. However, these pioneering initiatives are not often linked to a wider church community and therefore lack the necessary support. In turn the centre-church misses out on the inherent encouragement of the edge and of learning new ways of engagement.

Ten years ago, when Justin was appointed as the new Bishop of the Wellington diocese, he discovered the diocese had planted only two new parishes in the last 20 years. That rate of growth didn't even match the diocese's population growth and certainly didn't cater for the boom in new suburbs and city centres, never mind innovating to meet the needs of those leaving the diocese's traditional churches or attracting new spiritual seekers. Since becoming Bishop of the diocese Justin has set up a 'Pioneer Development Unit' which now mentors and supports five movements with apostolic and prophetic charisms, some with multiple teams on the ground. The good news is that these edge-dwellers' new initiatives and their apostolic-prophetic voices are influencing the whole diocese. Their exciting missional adventures are also helping to connect more people to established centre church life in the diocese: an encouragement for edge-dwellers and centre-church leaders alike.

We in the centre of established church life need the edge-dwellers to reincarnate a passionate gospel life that speaks to wider cultural needs and anxieties. We need them to identify the key areas of change which God is bringing and to live into this change. When they do this their faithfulness to a counter-cultural and passionate gospel lifestyle speaks to and exposes the wider church's idolatry. The models of gospel-living they create offer glimpses of how others in the centre-church can also reorient their lives, even in relatively small but targeted ways. This is powerful for the whole church, as the lived faithfulness of edge-dwellers challenges and shows a new way forward for centre-church leaders and people.

This process of change doesn't happen by reading books, nor by hearing or giving sermons. It doesn't happen through attending church, theological or local mission conferences, even the very best of these. If they were effective, we would have renewed the church years ago. Books, seminars and sermons are our most relied upon methods of discipleship and effecting change and as the church has declined over the last few decades the volume of these has exploded. The word must be made incarnate to bring change and new life. Where can we see the word incarnate? Where can we go to learn by experience?

The Wellington Anglican Diocese is experimenting with resourcing edge groups by welcoming them into protected space on the edge of its centre-churches, away from the core business of usual church life. The diocese is helping centre-church leaders understand the place of edge-dwellers, providing theological and biblical understandings for their role in reshaping church life. It is equipping and growing the apostles and pioneers, bringing them together with other like-minded communities at festivals and gatherings, which include a dedicated team who listen to, pray for and protect them. They need these spaces, training opportunities, and support people to allow them to be together, hone their skills, and be encouraged in their engagement with the wider church.

The diocese then takes the learnings and experiences of the passionate gospel-led lifestyles of the edge-dwellers back into centre-church leaders' gatherings and helps translate it for the wider church to learn from. Is this relationship full of tension? Of course, just as there are misunderstandings, hard words spoken, failures and mistakes. We believe this relationship, at its best, holds an inherent and natural level of tension which is healthy and necessary. When wholly engaged in the relationship, the centre-church leaders and centre-church people will be deeply challenged by the message and lifestyle of the prophets and apostolics.

There are some significant questions for edge-dwelling leaders to grapple with; are there emerging stories of God's grace at work in people's lives? Of people coming to faith in Jesus and expressing that faith with their friends? Of people sensing their deep pain being spoken to and their overwhelming fear being held in God's power? As Justin and Jenny look to the edge-dwellers they work with, they see that the answer is: yes, there are! These stories bring energy, hope, creativity and models for other apostolic and prophetic types but also for the wider church. Everyone can be encouraged!

Before we outline a model of how centre and edge can relate to, learn from and support one another, let's look back and see this dynamic at work in significant change points of the church's history.

Summary

❖ Centre-church must change in order to address people's personal pain, cultural angst and current forms of idolatry in the church. Current approaches and techniques are not working, and we need something fresh.

❖ The five-fold ministry described in Ephesians shows both a variety of leadership roles and giftings and necessitates them working together in a healthy tension for the health and growth of the church.

❖ Today most established centre-churches are led by pastors and teachers. While there are prophets, apostles and evangelists in leadership they are not prevalent in centre-church structures in the way they need to be.

❖ Centre-church leaders can invite edge-dwellers into a relationship where differences are recognised and respected without trying to bring the edge-dwellers under the church programmes and management.

❖ Edge-dwellers explore the unknown through different means to find needed resources for the whole community.

❖ Protestant practices of splitting to form the new and missiological frameworks that encourage separation are contrary to our suggested model of in-tensional relationship.

❖ The life of the Wellington Anglican diocese illustrates the dynamic, mutually transformative relationship that edge-dwellers and centre-church can form, without one being dominant.

Chapter 3 — Stories of Renewal

The good news is we've been here before. The church has navigated times of great cultural upheaval when its structures and practices were disconnected from the societal apprehensions of the time. In such times of societal crisis and church despondency, renewal movements arose and challenged existing church patterns, speaking directly to society's fears. These movements began in the hearts of dedicated and visionary followers of Christ who formed new models of gospel living for others to imitate. In this chapter we will unpack three eras of cultural change and emergent faith responses and list these renewal movements' common patterns.

To the desert

The early church was persecuted, small and struggling. The followers of Jesus were hated, misunderstood, ridiculed and looked down on. Both local authorities and the Roman Empire persecuted Christians, yet they continued to patiently live out their everyday faith. Although their meetings were closed and only for the baptised, their way of life was visible to all. They inspired those around them, drawing more and more people into their tight circle and the faith spread quietly from home to home, village to village, region to region. This slow spread changed suddenly when the Emperor Constantine became a Christian and made Christianity the religion of the Empire.

With the Emperor promoting the faith, Christians quickly moved from being outcasts to having influence at the very centre of the society, the economy and in politics. Christians who were once persecuted found themselves popular, their faith fashionable. They began enjoying the benefits of their new influence. Their new status attracted many others, people who would never have joined the persecuted, ridiculed and marginal Christian communities. New compromises and comforts became part of the Christian lifestyle, and the counter-cultural nature of the church communities was largely lost.

Into this compromised and societally acceptable church context stepped a wealthy young man named Anthony. Entering a church, he heard words that struck him deeply and fundamentally changed his life. The words were from Matthew's gospel: "If you would be perfect, go, sell what you possess and give to the poor and you will have treasure in heaven." Anthony sensed God was speaking to him and, following this call, he sold everything and left town to join a group of desert dwelling hermit Christians.

Anthony wasn't alone. Others also saw church leaders and church structures being compromised, as the newfound popularity was distorting the radical call of the gospel. Anthony and people like him rejected popularity for more radical lifestyles with greater gospel integrity. Many headed to the desert in a new style of martyrdom which meant rejecting comfort for deep commitment and a radical life for Christ. These new martyrs of Christ were not under threat of death, but they were giving up the comforts that Christian faith now offered. Many lived together, consuming only enough to survive while praying and worshipping God fervently. Slowly they created daily rhythms of prayer, silence, worship and work, forming a new, radical way of life for believers.

The desert movement began to catch on and soon thousands were following them. It wasn't just men adopting this lifestyle. Women responded to the same call by choosing a celibate life within their urban and family contexts. The records show very large numbers were involved; for example, by the end of the fourth century close to 5000 men lived around just one mountain and it was estimated there were 20,000 celibate Christian women in Egypt. What had begun as a break-away movement was itself gaining popularity.

It was primarily people like Anthony – the relatively wealthy and well connected – who heard this call and sought to radically reshape their lives. Many were people who naturally held social capital, people with a good education, social standing and some degree of wealth. But although they were privileged, they were deeply dissatisfied with the lifestyle of both their culture and the church. They carried a deep pain or angst that was only met in the call to reject career, power, family and social ties as well as the established and now powerful church of the empire.

The lifestyle of the desert dwelling radical Christians spoke powerfully to the deep cultural disquiet, underlying questions and concerns of the mainstream culture of the time. These were the days of Platonic idealism that praised the human desire to escape the material world for a more spiritual life. Desert Christians lived this fully with their total rejection of society and its values. Yet in adopting the desert lifestyle they were also deeply connected to the dominant Platonic value of the spiritual over the material. The desert lifestyle was seen to strip away the material world so they would experience the richness of the spiritual life. In this way, the desert radicals became a culturally relevant alternative to the mainstream culture.

Ironically, these desert radicals who turned their back on popular culture became popular. By their lifestyle, dedication to their faith and care of the poor many in the wider society saw them as gaining supernatural prestige and social standing. They gained wide influence and even a powerful voice within society, albeit far away in the deserts. Their perceived independence and spiritual depth meant they were popular as village mediators and for their advice and spiritual insight. Individual desert dwellers and their communities rose in popularity, which in turn increased their perceived holiness. As one's holiness increased, so the expectation to play an intercessory role on behalf of society rose. Far from being removed from society, the radical choice and consistent lifestyle of these desert-dwellers saw them drawn back into society and the church.

The desert dwellers had seen the church as compromised and abandoned it. As a lay movement, the desert Christians could be critical. They were not dependent on the church and received no support from the church structures; they were not accountable, nor looking to church leaders for oversight. They had an outsider's view. Their freedom and growing influence began to pose a problem for the church leaders as the desert dwellers were increasingly held up as saints. If their popularity was left unchecked their power and influence would eclipse that of the church. Some church leaders responded by attacking the desert dwellers, claiming they lived loose lives, bound to no authority and doing whatever they chose.

Other church leaders responded quite differently. Athanasius the Bishop of Alexandria saw the power of the desert movement and sought to reconnect it with the established church. He spent several years living with the desert Christians and sought to connect them back into the established church. Athanasius' solution was to write an account of Anthony's life. He knew doing so would effectively market the desert lifestyle to a wider audience and elevate its popularity. Through the biography he endorsed the movement and cleverly drew it back towards the established church.

Some desert leaders were also drawn back into the established church by accepting invitations to become priests in churches and even bishops. For example, Martin of Tours, a desert hermit, was made Bishop of Tours in 371AD. Athanasius' book, *Life of Saint Anthony* and the appointment of desert dwellers as church leaders started to connect the desert movement to the established church. This led to tensions as some desert Christians remained deeply sceptical of the church's motivations and encouraged even greater withdrawal into the desert.

A movement that started as a departure from society and established church began to influence and reshape the practices, teaching and structures of church, reshaping it in ways that enabled it to speak to and engage with the deep societal troubles of the day.

To the monastery

Turn the clock forward a few hundred years and the Roman Empire was crumbling; its internal social and political structures were strained and the so called 'Barbarians' were threatening to invade. A new era of instability, often called the Dark Ages, would envelop Europe for centuries as feudalism replaced the Roman Empire's rule. Feudal society in Europe was hierarchical, inherently unjust and violent.

A new form of Christian living took hold as monasteries began to emerge, offering a communal, disciplined way of life incorporating a daily rhythm of prayer and work. Compared to the chaos and violence of the feudal culture the monasteries were an oasis of order and stability. Monasteries established skilled work for the monks, such as baking, agricultural tasks, animal husbandry, bee keeping and brewing. There were also monastic roles focused on philosophy and all forms of art, on administrative law and financial specialities. As Friedrich Silbur states, the monasteries "served... as medieval equivalents of banks, hotels, old-age homes, and even asylums; they absorbed unmarried women of great families, cared for unwanted children... provided clerical help to princes... monasteries were... the main educational and intellectual institutions".[10]

The monasteries lived by a rule of life. These rules set down processes for accepting new people to the communal life, periods of probation before taking vows, and ways to care for all community members including the elderly and sick. Leaders were chosen from within the community and provided clear structures for living faithfully together. With these rules, the monasteries didn't need exceptional leaders because average leaders could effectively manage a monastery by the book. This simple leadership structure enabled more and more monasteries to be established across Europe.

Many wanted to join the monastic life and the Augustine and Benedictine orders were very attractive. Personal spiritual development was a strong motivation, but the opportunity to learn a craft, live in a stable community, and be freed from feudal violence and societal demands were also appealing. For many male aristocrats, monastic life offered safe refuge from the political turmoil and dangers of the time. For women, the monastery offered a positive and empowering alternative lifestyle without pressure to marry or raise a family. They could be self-supporting, gain an education, live with other women, and take on leadership or administrative roles – all unavailable to them outside the monastery.

The monasteries were powerful institutions in European society for over a thousand years. They effectively nurtured the Christian faith of those committed to the monastic life and offered intercessory services and worship for the wider society. They also cared for the poor, provided education, nurtured the arts and became integral and significant societal forces.

The monastic movement was both an alternative to cultural norms and critical of the dominant culture. But it also spoke convincingly to the cultural needs of the time, particularly the needs for stability, education, spiritual development, learning and law and order. For many they were a type of utopia offering a certainty in an age of great flux and instability. One of the key building blocks of the Rule of Benedict was the vow of stability. This vow drew adherents to commit to one community and vocation for the whole of their lives and spoke deeply to the societal angst in a culture of chaos and violence.

The Monastics also spoke through their non-violent lifestyle which provided a critique to the endemic violence of feudal society. In its day, monasticism was seen as a 'peace of God' movement offering protection to the poor and most vulnerable. In addition, monks provided prayerful intercession and spiritual services to those in the wider society, especially kings and powerful landowners. In exchange, they often received material support and gifts of land.

Like the desert dwellers, the Monastic movement clearly contrasted with both societal and clerical lifestyles. The monasteries' financial independence and lay leadership allowed them some distance from diocesan influence. A dance between church and monastic leaderships began around who had the greatest influence and control in the wider communities. History shows an ebb and flow in both directions, but the influence of the monasteries slowly grew. Their popularity with the people coupled with stability, education and service to the least gave them huge influence in villages, towns and even in national decisions.

What began as a small breakaway movement of lay people, protesting the dominant culture yet faithfully upholding core gospel values, became attractive and ended up influencing church and popular culture.

To the beggars

By the 13th century change was again afoot in European society. Feudalism was crumbling and both the established church and many monasteries were showing signs of internal corruption, compromise and a loss of passion for the gospel. A spirit of individualism permeated society and a powerful and wealthy urban elite were emerging.

Into this context two key Christians, Francis and Dominic, began new alternative movements of radically lived Christian faith. Francis, born in 1181, was raised the son of a wealthy textile merchant. As a care-free youth he dreamt of becoming a knight, fighting mighty crusades, rescuing damsels in distress and spending his time with friends. But then, in 1209, this wealthy playboy heard the words of Matthew 10:9. This verse speaks of leaving gold, silver or copper behind and doing the work of Christ empty-handed. In a radical response to the passage, Francis dedicated his life to the pursuit of the Kingdom of God and to the service of 'Lady Poverty'.

A small group of other wealthy young men joined him. They lived very simply, wearing only coarse garments, begging for their food, turning their back on wealth and preaching in the new urban centres.

Dominic was born nine years before Francis, and after an extensive education he began a career in the church. By 25 he was committed to the rule of St Augustine and had risen in the church hierarchy. Acutely aware of the rising heresies in the church, Dominic committed himself to preaching and poverty which he saw as a pragmatic response. He soon gathered others around him: a small band committed to a lifestyle of poverty and preaching.

The followers of Francis and Dominic, known as the Franciscans and Dominicans respectively, were mendicants, meaning they lived by begging for their support. They would go wherever Christ led them, taking no gold or silver but depending on God through people's gifts. Unlike the now wealthy and established monasteries these mendicants focused on preaching, begging, and living in the growing urban areas. They insisted on begging for their needs so their preaching would have credibility.

They desired to live fully committed to the heart of the gospel, offering a radical alternative to both church and society. Their lifestyle made a strong statement and as society's wealth gap increased, others were drawn to follow. Paradoxically, it was not the destitute who embraced the vow, but rather the wealthy and the rising middle class.[11] The Franciscan and Dominican orders allowed married people, those with families, agricultural workers, and servants to join. These they called the third level orders. Within the Franciscans, for example, the first order was for men who had left everything to follow Jesus. The second order was for women who had also chosen a lifestyle based on the same vows, for example the order of the Poor Clares.

While first and second orders took a vow of celibacy, third order Franciscans could marry and continue their prior work while still following the ways of the order, enabling many more people to participate.

Francis and his followers offered a stark alternative to the cultural norms of their day. Within the remnants of feudal society, which prized greatness, Francis humbly called himself the 'lesser brother'. Within an emerging society based on wealth, Francis identified with absolute poverty, and he chose to be a lay person within the hierarchical church. It was a deeply spiritual and highly attractive alternative within Europe's new urban moneyed societies.

At the time of the Franciscans and the Dominicans many small groups sought to live alternative expressions of Christian faith but most disappeared, having failed to attract followers. What helped the Franciscans grow and become an enduring order? Francis understood his call from God as not his alone but rather a treasure of the church to be shared widely. So, he sought authentication for his fledgling movement from Pope Innocent III.

Francis critiqued the clericalism of monastic life and the church's paternalism and feudalism, and his vow of absolute poverty was a clear critique of the indulgent lifestyles of many in the church, which at the time owned half the land in Europe. In seeking the Pope's endorsement for his new community, Francis desired loyalty to the church while prophetically calling people to a passionate life of gospel expression. Francis' unique brilliance was not so much his breakaway lifestyle and beliefs, but his ability to remain within, and offer this charism to, the wider church.

The desert dwellers, early monastics and mendicants are examples of three radical Christian movements which shaped the church and society of their day. From our perspective today, we may overlook the tension that existed between the established church and these movements. The established church leaderships didn't accept these movements until they saw their positive influence on the population and how their lives of Christian faithfulness spoke to the great cultural questions and fears of the day. When the church leaders listened to the breakaway groups, they did not wholly embrace their charisms, nor did they become part of the movements or encourage their congregations to do so. Yet they did endorse those called to these new expressions of Christian faith, and they incorporated elements of their practice into their churches.

From these incorporated practices and by bringing some leaders from the new movements into leadership roles in the church hierarchy, small but significant changes were brought into the established church. Many still have an influence today, like the daily office, born out of monastic prayer rhythms, or the third order

Franciscans who could be deeply committed to Franciscan values while being actively involved in society and the church.

We have named three large, well-researched, epoch-shaping movements, but there were many other movements that followed similar patterns, each helping to bridge the gap between the established church and wider cultural concerns, questions and social unease. Justin has often been asked to speak on this and to help illustrate he has drawn the following image.

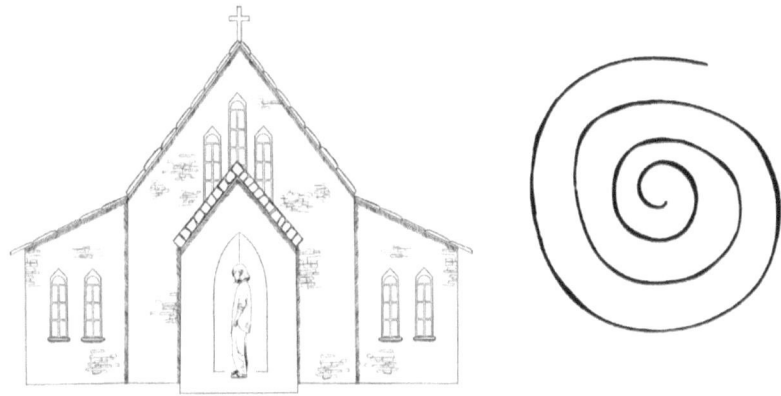

In this diagram the church is on the left with its straight lines, solid form and highly identifiable cross on top. On the right, the spiral, with its curves and inherent movement depicts the wider community. These shapes illustrate the gap between an institutional, structured and established church and the unfolding, spiralling cultural context we live in.

Using these two images, Justin describes the historical moments when the church found itself out of alignment with wider society. Times when society changed and moved while the church remained static, gradually separating from societies' needs and from radical expressions of gospel life. He argues that today the west is in one of these moments, where the church is not a living presence of salt and light for a new generation. The western church has become compromised, idolatrous and insipid. The good news is God has a renewal plan.

In the image below we have placed the three movements on the spiral as indicators of new expressions which resonated naturally and deeply with the issues, questions and hungers of their time.

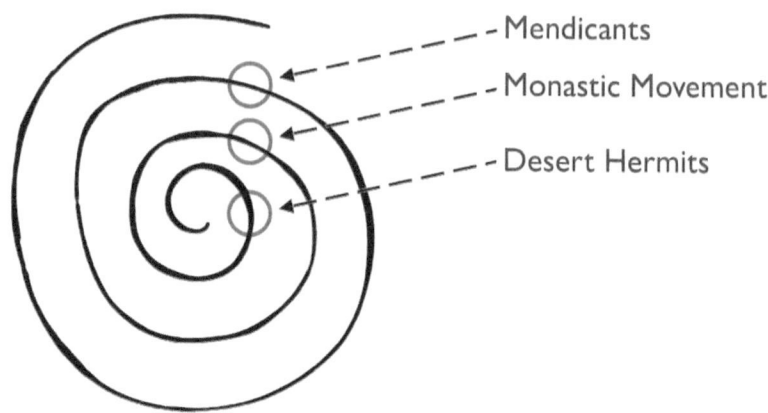

These movements are illustrative; we could easily tell the story of Ignatius of Loyola who started the Jesuit order with just 10 followers. Or in a New Zealand context, the prophetic pioneer Suzanne Aubert who after decades of struggle and loyal service to the church began the Sisters of Mercy which prioritised working with Māori and the poor, seeking justice for women and care of orphaned children. There are also the Wesleyans, the Salvation Army, the Moravians and more recently the Vineyard movement. These were all radical communities expressing the gospel in relevant ways.

Christian history reveals critical tipping points where we see a compromised church, lacking deep commitment to Christ and mission. In these moments new movements emerge as God calls people to a radical outworking of Christian faith. This new way of life powerfully responds to societies' angst and hunger, providing places where people can commit their lives fully to Christ, serving the greatest needs of the day. The group's members intuitively respond to what God desires within the world. If these groups learn to sustain themselves, and the wider church appreciates them, great renewal can come. The church can repent of its idolatry, embracing a deep fidelity to Christ and becoming a contagious vehicle of the good news of Jesus.

In all the historical movements of God, prophetic and apostolic edge-dwellers have been at the forefront. Over time others join them and communities are formed. The early leaders train many new leaders, so that the movement can grow without a focus on a particular charismatic leader or group of leaders. With the growth of the new movement and its increasing popularity the church is changed and called back to the heart of the gospel. However, this is only possible if the centre church and edge groups build influential relationships, allowing renewal to flow between them.

Patterns of new movements that take root

The movements begin with radicals. Hearing the word 'radical', we can tend to think 'extreme' but the word radical also means to come back or return to the beginnings of something. Naming the early leaders of these movements 'radicals' reminds us of their uncompromising lifestyle that returned them to the roots of the gospel. Max Weber, a founder of Sociology, called such radicals 'Religious Virtuosi', meaning they live a particular virtue of Christian faith with such deep and uncompromising commitment that it contrasts sharply with society's emptiness and the church's unfaithfulness.

Typically, the radical leaders are lay people rather than existing church leaders. Because of this they have more freedom but are at first disregarded within the church.

For the movement to survive and instigate change it must connect deeply with a powerful underlying angst or desire in the wider society by grasping a gospel imperative in a fresh way. The lived gospel expression of the new radicals must both critique the wider culture and be a radical alternative to it.

Typically, these first radicals come from amongst the influential and wealthy of society. They lay down their personal social capital to follow their sense of call to serve the poor and marginalised. Most are lay people from outside the church hierarchy.

For these radical movements to grow they must move beyond the pioneer phase and allow the essence (charism) of their radicalness to be institutionalised. The movement must become explainable and transferable so it can be widely adopted. This process of routinisation allows ordinary leaders – not only exceptional leaders – to carry the movement forward.

These radical pioneers and the movements they begin are recognised and supported by the wider church which embraces them without making the wider church adopt their expression of gospel life; a brave move on behalf of the church hierarchy as radicals often point out the church's flaws. The new radicals need to be willing to engage with the church leadership and to return to, or stay within, the church family. The growth and health of a new radical movement relies on it influencing the wider church and being supported by it.

God has renovated his church through this process many times in the past and we believe God is doing this again today: that God is raising up new prophetic, pioneering, entrepreneurial, radical gospel-livers whose commitments and passion offer another way to both the established church and our wider communities.

Chapter 4 — So, What Do We Do?

The church in the west is declining at a critical rate, due largely to its lack of alignment with the heart of the gospel at this time in history. We have become flabby, idolatrous and compromised, out of touch with people's pain and our deepest cultural longings and angst. In the previous chapter we explored how past apostolic and prophetic leaders – edge leaders – have sensed the call to a new radical way of gospel-faithfulness. Some of the alternative expressions of faith, and the communities they created, have become beacons of hope, speaking to the very heart of people's deep pain. When the centre-church can integrate them into the wider life of the church, it has been able to bring renewal and change. We can learn from this history, but it is a delicate dance for centre-church and radical edge-leaders to do this well.

What now?

Let's use a parable, with alternate endings, to illustrate. This parable is dramatised and intentionally extreme in its characterization, to identify the dynamics at play.

A young woman called Mia has recently come to faith and is well connected in societal culture beyond Christian sub-culture and church practice. Mia has a deep desire to see her friends and people like them come to know Jesus and to share the faith that she has found. Mia is bold, opinionated and confident. A clear leader. Imagine Mia comes to the attention of a centre-church leadership who decide to encourage and support her.

Some people will feel uncomfortable with having Mia in their church. She didn't grow up in a church family and is a newcomer. She has a fresh perspective, and while she's passionate about her new faith and desperately wants to share it with her friends, she is critical of the way the church operates. Some of it doesn't make sense to her and some of it feels alienating or even discriminatory to her and her friends. Her criticisms could include any of the following: the worship is out of touch, the church doesn't seem to reflect God's concern for the poor, the all-white male leadership lacks ethnic and gender inclusion, the church services don't encourage diverse voices and perspectives, there's no focus on the impacts of climate change or concern for millions of people who will become climate change refugees. The list could go on.

Mia fears her friends would never feel comfortable in the church and the church doesn't reach out to them anyway. She has experienced the transforming power of God and reads about it in the Bible but doesn't see it at work in the church. The regular church members seem to be no different than the average member of society. As she puts it: their lives look like they follow 'House and Garden' more than the Bible. To Mia church seems all hype and little substance, with no depth of contemplation or commitment. Mia is dissatisfied because she knows intuitively that the people she cares about are never going to connect with the expression of Christian faith she sees at church.

Now imagine that you, as part of the centre-church leadership, recognise Mia's strong opinions about the issues she has raised. Her deep desire for change could be centred around homelessness, climate change, global violence, lack of healthcare options for the marginalised, lack of connection with our elders, child poverty, the place of our indigenous people in society or a more radical expression of evangelism, healing, contemplative worship or prophetic expression. Whatever her concern she is sure the church is missing the point. She relates well to people outside the church and naturally draws people around her. If you see she has leadership potential even if you don't agree with her analysis of the church; what should you do?

Consider the diagram from the previous chapter. On the left a drawing (all straight lines and right angles) of a building with a cross represents a stereotypical centre-church. The spiral on the right is circular with flowing movement which expands outwards. The spiral encapsulates our wider culture's life and expression of deepest need and spiritual distress. The church, on the left, is shown as isolated from and closed off from this wider culture. The juxtaposition of these images illustrates the enormous gap and fundamental difference between church and the societal culture we live in.

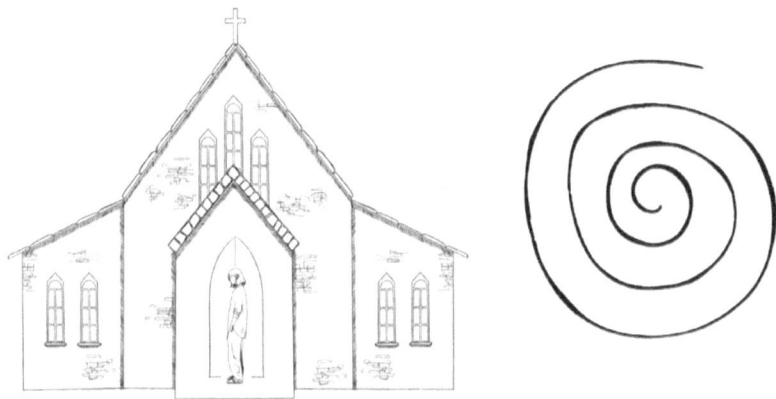

Using this diagram we suggest that edge-dwellers, like Mia fit comfortably and naturally into the spiral image on the right and centre-church leaders in the stereotypical church on the left. Mia intuitively speaks and embodies the language of contemporary culture and can articulate God's heart response to this culture's deepest angst. Centre-church leaders by training and socialisation are fluent in the language of church but at best, contemporary culture is their second language. Centre-church leaders will probably never be fluent in contemporary culture, and they need Mia to be their guide. Here's the first version of Mia's story.

The Usual Tale

When Mia approaches centre-church leaders with her idea to reach out to a particular people group or start a mission venture, this is what normally happens. Centre-church leaders encourage Mia in her leadership gifts by saying, "we think your ideas are 'interesting' and your faith and commitment to Jesus excite us. We see your potential to influence the church and suggest you start by serving as a volunteer youth leader. It's a chance for us to get to know each other and for you to prove yourself. As a youth leader you can explore your ideas around the issues you have raised. Once a term you could lead the youth group to reach out to the people or need you have identified. But please remember, our teenagers also need encouragement and support, and other youth leaders have different passions". The centre-church leadership tempers Mia's passion while keeping the youth group programme 'safe' for centre-church teens and parents.

Mia proves herself as a great volunteer youth leader. A few months in she has worked hard and won the leaders' trust to such a degree that they encourage the church leadership to take her on as youth pastor. The church leadership are excited, reassuring Mia that she can keep exploring the issues she's passionate about, but suggesting she tread carefully, as some parents are concerned about her 'radical', even 'dangerous' ideas. The leaders explain the importance of slowly winning the teens and their parents' trust before implementing anything too drastic.

Two years later Mia has built considerable trust with her youth and their parents and the church leaders now offer her a different role in the church as a worship leader or a regular preacher. In time this new role will give her more influence to develop her 'interesting' ideas and her growing trust with the church will enable her passions to be picked up by others. However, the leaders remind her, the church is diverse and it's important in her new role to serve the whole church, rather than pushing her personal bandwagon. The leaders explain that with input into her new area, the church could grow significantly, bringing more people who Mia can influence.

Down the track, church members recognise Mia's giftedness and commitment. They want to support her, suggesting God has big plans for her future and the church leadership suggest she gets a theology degree. This will take three years, but the church can help with some costs, and everyone will encourage her and pray for her. Studying theology will broaden her theological understanding, strengthen her leadership and introduce her to other young leaders with similar 'interesting ideas'. After her studies she can reflect more deeply on the issues and ideas on her heart, and really invest in her dreams.

Mia does well at theological college and is offered a role in another church of the same denomination. Over the next two years Mia will learn how to run a whole church. The members of her home church are delighted by this exciting opportunity to deepen her leadership experience. Mia is encouraged to buckle down and learn the fundamentals; soon she will lead her own church and implement her ideas.

With the best intent and expectations, the centre-church leaders around Mia supported her, encouraged her, gave money and provided opportunities to help her grow as a leader. They see Mia as a significant part of the hope of the next generation. The centre-church leaders had been praying for new leaders, and Mia is now equipped, theologically educated, trained and ready. She is grateful for the mentoring, opportunities and support from centre-church leaders.

Soon Mia will be free to lead her own church as she senses God is leading her. But for now, she fits the mould of centre-church life and is preoccupied with the busy day-to-day stuff of running a church. Finally, the day arrives, and Mia is ready to be a senior pastor or vicar. Praise God! The church which needs innovative and passionate young leadership to face an unknown future now has Mia to help lead the way. Surely this has been a success.

When Justin tells this story to groups of church leaders, theological students or within church communities he ends by asking, "but what has happened to Mia?"

The response is always pretty much the same. As one young leader answered dejectedly, "Mia has got old". Mia is probably still only in her thirties, however, at a deeper level she has become part of the old ways. Part of the establishment. Church leadership is demanding and time consuming. She has probably lost connection with her initial sense of passion and the calling she had, and certainly has lost contact with her friends outside the church who shared her passionate concerns for a gospel expression outside centre-church.

Let's illustrate this journey. This diagram is thanks to Dave Andrews who first drew our attention to this dynamic. As Dave says, every organisation, including the church, is basically a hierarchy where the further up you go in the leadership, the more you are shaped by the organisation, (church or denomination) that you are part of. Mia has naturally been offered the next steps of responsibility and leadership as she climbed the leadership ladder of her church.

In the diagram below we see that Mia has climbed the leadership ladder at the centre of the established church structures. Each step required an element of indoctrination and domestication to the dominant centre-church culture and paradigm. To a prophetic or apostolic leader, each step meant compromise in their missional passion, vision of hope and prophetic voice. Each step meant becoming more fluent in the language of the church and thereby often forgetting the language and concerns of contemporary culture.

Finally, Mia, the passionate young prophet and radical entrepreneur, reaches a place of influence in the church, but she no longer has anything unique to offer. The church has lost her most precious gift at a time it needed it most. She has become an old leader in a young body. Although Mia outwardly looks like she will push for change, she has become enculturated in the status quo. Mia could have brought the voice and freshness of a new generation but she has become disconnected from the margins, losing her critical perspective and/or the means and will to implement it.

Mia now naturally incarnates the values of the established church structure. While the church believes it has fresh innovative leadership, it has in fact indoctrinated Mia. This is not all bad for the church. In Mia it has a young, stable and newly accredited leader, but it has probably lost the opportunities for entrepreneurial initiatives in new areas. The connection to people beyond the centre-church catchment and Mia's high-commitment to critical issues have been lost.[12]

The Unusual Tale

If elements of Mia's story resonate with your experience of centre-church and how young, inexperienced, culture-savvy, passionate, prophetic and apostolic leaders are drawn into existing church paradigms, then you understand our crucial question. How could we do it differently? When we come across a radical like Mia, with strong ideas and leadership potential, what is the alternative pathway?

Instead of asking Mia to contribute her leadership and energy into the church's existing programmes, let's encourage her to shift to the inside-edge of the church (see diagram below): inside the church but not pushed to climb the ladder in the centre.

What if the centre-church leaders encouraged Mia, from the beginning, to try making her passion a lived reality. The centre-church leaders could say: "If you believe strongly in reaching people like yourself, create an alternative which reflects what you think God is inviting us into". Mia would need to draw a team together with the church leadership's encouragement and backing.

In the diagram below we show Mia's pilot project at the edge of the church, hopefully with greater freedom to respond in a gospel way to her sense of cultural angst. The cloud with the dark outline represents the gospel expression that Mia believes could draw people into an experience of Jesus.

There are advantages for everyone in keeping Mia's pilot project on the edge. Those she wants to reach don't see Mia as too close to the church they may have already rejected, instead they experience Mia and her team's concern for them. For the church there are advantages too. Mia's project is not part of the church's programmes: it doesn't need approval to begin and doesn't need to follow church protocols. If the experiment is a spectacular failure, the risks to the church are minimised, and the central structure and life of the church isn't disturbed. The church has plausible deniability of ownership and responsibility.

This diagram shows that it's easy for the church to cut Mia off if necessary. If church leadership is willing to relinquish control of Mia's movement, then they could legitimately say they supported the experiment but looking at its path, have decided not to pursue it further. This potential cutting off is not a bad thing for Mia. If the church leaders have greater control, then any decisions about the group's future will be according to the centre-church leaders' sense of what is right. Inevitably Mia will have little space to innovate.

On the edge Mia has the freedom to make calls without being controlled or potentially upsetting others in the church. She can make her own decisions and has the space she needs from church leadership structures and particular groups within the church who may feel threatened by her ideas. At the same time, she has the unofficial support of key centre-church leaders.

If over time Mia and her team create a positive alternative that is offering a unique expression of gospel life to the community, then the centre-church leaders can say, "we have been following and quietly supporting Mia and her team. This could be an important part of our church life too". This allows the centre-church community to be influenced by the new life at its edge.

Diagrammatically, if Mia's group mature well, creating something that is fruitful, smells of the Kingdom and has moved to a sustainable model, then the whole experiment can stretch the church.

Being on the edge gives Mia a few other advantages that increase the likelihood of her mission venture succeeding. The church should not help fund the new venture and therefore cannot expect to have control over or influence in any decision making. Money always comes with strings: the need to show outcomes and provide reports, the need to comply with church guidelines and protocols and, almost inevitably, the need to give back to the centre-church as well as developing the new entrepreneurial initiative.

If Mia's team really believes in their call, they will manage with their own resources and the personal sacrifices they choose to make. The outcome will generally be richer because of this freedom and personal commitment. Having financial distance from the church will be good for Mia's discipleship journey. She must depend on God to provide in tangible ways. She may have to work part-time and sacrifice other culturally encouraged agendas like buying a house, getting an education or travelling. It sounds harsh, but it is trusting the wisdom of Gamaliel who is recorded in Acts 5 as saying 'if it's of God it will begin to flourish'. Centre-church leaders and congregations naturally reach to offer financial support, but offering money too soon is more of a hindrance than a support.

By encouraging Mia to move to the edge of the church, she will have the time, freedom and opportunity to develop a new mission venture or community initiative. Mia will need a team of people around her who believe in the same cause she does. This team understands the issue from the inside and has the capacity and will to be part of creating an alternative. The new work is something the church leaders can encourage and pray for, while not being directly involved. This doesn't mean Mia should be left alone. She needs the support of others and specifically she will need a sponsor and a mentor. These roles are quite different, and they need to be provided by different people.

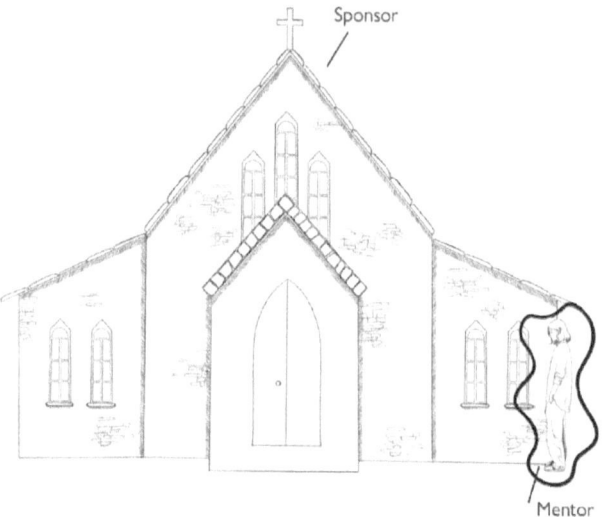

Mia's sponsor will be someone who is an integral part of the church leadership and can back and support her. The sponsor would not belong to Mia's group. They don't need to understand or agree with what Mia's group is trying. But they do need to have a sense that God is in Mia's particular calling and have some personal experience of prophetic and apostolic groups.

The sponsor ensures Mia's is encouraged and protected and provides a wise sounding board when necessary. Their role is critically important, protecting Mia's prototype group from being controlled, diluted or vigorously questioned too early in the mission venture's establishment. If people in the church start murmuring about Mia's radical experiment, calling it dangerous, heretical, outside church protocol, or even begin undermining her, then her sponsor can protect her behind the scenes. This protection gives Mia the space she needs to experiment without undue interruption or opposition.

The sponsor fights Mia's institutional battles leaving Mia free to focus her energies on creating an alternative gospel-reality rather than being taken up by church politics or satisfying the church leadership needs. Her most precious resource – time – is voluntary, and she's giving it in pursuit of a difficult, but Godly dream. Let the sponsor, who is already trusted and part of the church leadership, have the conversations and report to the boards to keep the institutional side of centre-church happy.

Mia and her team also need a good mentor. Normally this mentor is from outside the centre-church. Mia and her team's new initiative may involve people, groups or activities that the mentor is not familiar with. That is OK. What the mentor brings is experience leading a prior pioneering mission venture that was risky and entrepreneurial in its own day. The mentor, like Mia, will have a strong prophetic and/or apostolic gifting. This person has learnt the leadership, missiological and sustainability lessons that only those experienced in the pioneering leadership space can offer. While the centre-church can help Mia find a mentor she can relate to and trust, the centre-church cannot often fill this role.

Centre-church leadership should give Mia and her team time to focus and grow something new, which takes time, dedicated effort, and a lot of encouragement. Pioneering is as demanding as leading a church with diverse pastoral needs, compliance requirements, unending expectations and denominational challenges. Knowing this, don't distract Mia and her team with invitations to be involved in other church activities and leadership opportunities. Don't expect them to be at church services every week or even every month. Simply ask that Mia and her team connect as much as they need to, which will be less than what others in the church suggest is necessary. Don't try to measure success or find the fruit too soon. The new roots won't grow if you're always digging the new plant up to see how much they've grown.

Centre-church leaders and the wider church community need to expect failures, disappointments and struggle. Consider the advice of Patricia Wittberg as she closes her book *Pathways to Re-creating Religious Communities*: "Expect to fail. Expect to fail several times. Expect to lose your way, to forget essential supplies, to suffer breakdowns (and breakups), to journey painstakingly for years only to face dead-ends and washed-out roads. Even if the larger congregation mentors your attempt, if they publicize your experiment and recruit new members for you, if they challenge you when you stray from your ideals and encourage you when you return to them – and this is precisely the role which established congregations should be playing to support their members' various refounding attempts – you will, quite possibly, still fail. Learn from your mistakes and try again... and again. That is what founders and refounders do. That is the crucifixion, the 'Passover', to which they are called. The resurrection, we know by faith, will also occur."[13]

If the centre church can support Mia and her team in these ways, they may create a vital new expression of gospel life. Sometimes, despite the best efforts, their attempt will fail, or produce little lasting fruit. This is the fragile nature of apostolic pioneering. Yet despite the fragility of Mia's new initiative, it may be the very thing God uses to offer a new picture of His Kingdom coming which can then encourage the whole church. It can inspire other new ventures and it seeds a culture which says, 'we don't have to do church the way we've always done it'. New initiatives and ventures are being raised up by the Holy Spirit and our church is part of that journey.

Mia and her team's venture may take root and engage deeply with a particular cultural pain or angst. Whichever journey Mia and her team walk, it is a success. Even when it fails miserably, its very existence says we are a church that allows experimentation. We want entrepreneurial prophets and apostles to try things and centre-church will do our part to help them. Everyone will learn important lessons and God can use the experience gained in another venture.

If Mia's new dream is fruitful and becomes a sustainable expression of God's Kingdom coming in fresh ways, then with careful integration, it can influence and renew the centre-church. This is the story of church history. When a church or denomination finds itself at a moment of crisis and opportunity, realising change is imperative, it begins to look for alternatives. Maybe these crucial moments don't require us to look far. If there is something fruitful and vibrant happening on the edge, the whole church can embrace some of the life this new movement is offering.

The diagram below shows aspects of Mia's initiative influencing centre church in different ways and in different parts of the centre-church life.

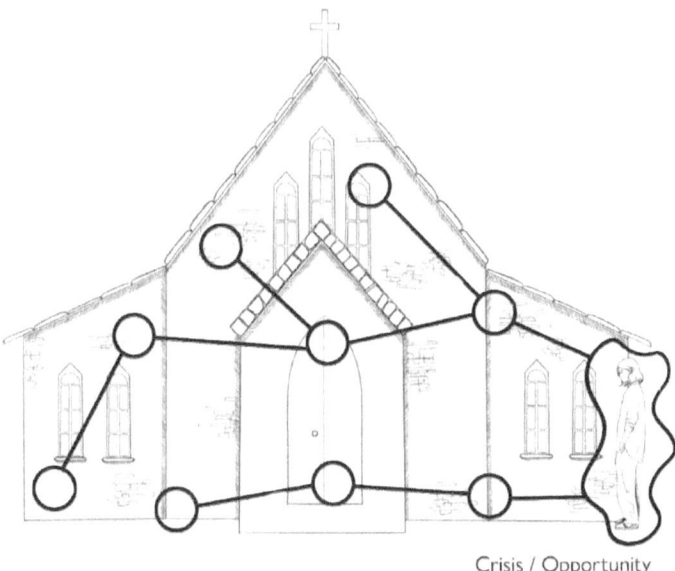

Crisis / Opportunity

When the centre-church is seeking new direction and vision it will be most interested in learning from Mia. It's not likely the church will suddenly replicate Mia's initiative, transplanting it from the edge directly into the centre of church life. But, as the following diagram illustrates, with wise integration, some of Mia and her team's passion, commitment, and innovations can be embraced by the whole church.

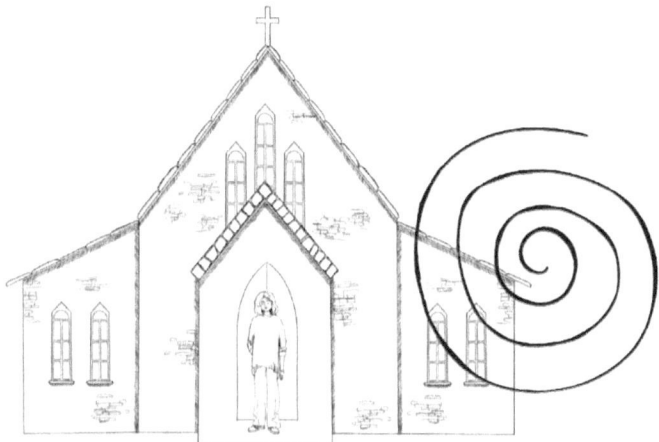

The centre-church – so often stuck in its existing patterns – can gradually incorporate Mia's new community gospel initiative into the wider church life. Now church members can begin to endorse Mia's venture and learnings and re-prioritise their own lives in line with the new community's example. Mia's passion and commitment to gospel faithfulness will also influence the congregation. By osmosis people will be encouraged to deeper faith, a higher spiritual temperature and a gospel that offers hope to the world.

Summary

❖ We have looked at two scenarios that a prophetic/apostolic leader with strong ties to cultural angst and wider societal life might be offered: first, the typical path where a Mia type leader is pulled into the needs, opportunities and leadership of central church. Second, an encouragement to start something outside the structures and responsibilities of the church, but close enough to be known and informally supported by centre-church leaders.

❖ Whatever the potential apostolic leader's passion (the poor, a commitment to deeper community belonging, a more radical reading of scripture) the important thing is to support them to make a start, build a team and learn from giving their all to what they sense God is leading them into.

❖ There are two central support roles an entrepreneurial edge-leader like Mia might need: a sponsor from within the church, and a mentor experienced in edge-leadership, probably from outside the church community.

❖ If the new gospel expression is positive the whole church can pivot in line with this life-giving direction bringing gospel life back into a fading church.

❖ This is how a centre-church could move towards greater alignment with the spiritual angst and needs of its culture; how a flabby, idolatrous and compromised church could be renewed.

❖ This story has many commonalities with historical church renewals and with our own experiences of the impact of edge-communities. We believe it is one of the important ways God is bringing new life and direction to his church.

Chapter 5 — What Edge and Centre Offer

In this chapter we will highlight the roles of edge and centre when they are at their best, in an ongoing conversation with each other, though reality will always be more complex and probably less positive than our description.

An in-tensional conversation is a deep dive into an on-going conversation that demands the full engagement of both centre-church and edge-church. It's a give and take relationship where both gain important learnings for the way forward. An in-tensional conversation is based on both edge and centre knowing who they are, what they offer, their strengths and their areas of weakness.

What the Edge Offers

The edge offers a living example of a highly committed expression of following Jesus and a deep and holistic commitment to the gospel. At their best, they live their faith energetically and are clearly focused on how the norms of wider society become idolatrous in our lives. The wider church, with its widespread compromise and nominalism needs the edge's wholehearted commitment and the prophetic imagination and apostolic vigour they bring is essential for church renewal.

Like most Christians, edge-dwellers believe the gospel calls us to surrender everything we are and have to the Lordship of Jesus and the work of the gospel. They passionately embody these beliefs, choosing to live a surrendered life in costly and highly committed counter-cultural ways. They want to bring gospel renewal in their community now and value this purposeful way of life as something to get up for each day. They have a singularity of effort because they are convinced by their sense of call and vision for change. Many have had a simple direct encounter; like that of Anthony or Dominic or Benedict, before them. A clear revelation where they sensed Jesus was speaking to them personally and a radical response was required. They believe their call is essential and their dream is the most important thing God is doing right now. Hence, they respond with energy, enthusiasm, love and action.

They are willing to pay a cost. It may begin with a naïve optimism, and some will give up when the lifestyle gets too demanding, but many remain, giving their time, using their skills, spending their cash, and choosing a life with less. If responding to climate change is their thing, they will boycott plastic, swap their car for a bike, refuse to fly, protest and campaign outside parliament and implore the church to recycle, reuse, compost, and care. They will feel disillusioned by anything that feels like a distraction or a compromise. It may be hard for them to talk, pray or think about anything else.

They probably won't be paid for the time or effort they put in and accept the need to earn an income elsewhere. Their cause is more important than a wage and committed volunteerism is the norm on the edge. They may be willing to sacrifice modern western capitalist idols of career, possessions, higher education and owning a home. They will willingly pay other prices too, like personal status, the understanding of friends and family and the loss of financial security. Edge-dwellers don't aspire to the social status of buying in the 'right' neighbourhood with 'good' schools or a secure superannuation plan. They likely feel uncomfortable about the possibility of being seen as successful. They would rather stay away from compromises, hints of hypocrisy or becoming part of the system.

When Justin illustrates these strengths of the edge-dwellers, through the journey of Urban Vision, he highlights how people have found creative ways to make a living while keeping their priority on the vision they feel called to. Some have job-shared, reduced income or sacrificed opportunities for promotion to enable them time to be present in their neighbourhoods and households. If they are studying, they may take fewer papers, accept lower grades and stretch out the time to complete their qualification so they can spend more time in their youth or community work. Others postpone buying a home, purchase a home in poorer communities or in worse condition or buy as a collective. Some take evening jobs so couples can juggle care of the children they foster after school. Behind each of these choices is an underlying critique of the societal expectation of 'getting ahead'.

Justin remembers one young member of an Urban Vision team who was incensed when the City Council bolted metal arm rests on the benches in the neighbouring park to prevent homeless people from sleeping on them. Without hesitation she unscrewed them. A see-sawing game between her and the council, screwing and unscrewing the arm rests, continued until she was arrested. That encouraged her to approach the media, telling them that providing somewhere for the homeless to lie down was something a caring community would do. With her passion, vision and single focus came the preparedness to grab her screwdriver and unscrew the arm rests, with the inherent risk of being arrested and potentially convicted for her actions.

To the surprise of edge-dwellers, centre-church leaders often see what can be done through the lens of budget realities and the need to keep donors and church members on side. A centre-church leader might say "we must work within the budget and sadly we don't have enough funding to pay someone to do this; it just can't happen". Edge-dwellers aren't shackled by the need for a wage or keeping to a timesheet. If something needs to be done, they will pay the price in lost income or extra hours. This collision of perspectives can be confronting and positive for church leaders and church structures. Churches are shrinking, congregations are ageing, living costs are rising and maintaining old buildings is costly. The edge-dwellers' courageous and creative approaches challenge centre-church limitations and encourage alternative ways to get stuff done without depleting the church's remaining resources.

Not being constrained by shrinking resources gives edge dwellers a way to multiply their work through inspiring others to join them. Because edge groups attract and link in people, including those who might struggle to find employment, they can grow the team from groupings in society that would not apply for or win paid roles. These may be people with significant personal struggles, little education or personal instability. In edge communities they are included and add to the diversity and strength of the team.

Edge communities attract prophetic people and often form questioning communities that love to face the complex issues of our time, think deeply and are willing to critique assumptions. They are repelled by the greed and self-centredness in society, and are constantly critiquing centre-church. They respond to what the centre-church may see as common-sense decisions with comments like 'what the hell?' and 'surely not'. They hear a centre-church say, 'it's the way we've always done it', and think 'yes, but it's not the way we have to keep on doing it'. They see what is broken, don't accept stagnation, and approach them differently. For them traditions need to be reconsidered in the light of new cultural realities and pains. Edge-dwellers bring new insight to blind-spots by pulling existing assumptions apart in search of the kernel of truth.

Unbeknown to many centre-church leaders the critique of the edge-dwellers is a gift. Their comments may hurt but they often represent the thoughts of the wider community whose perspective of church and Christian faith is seldom heard within centre-church. It's critical for centre-church to hear the perspective of the wider culture. Edge-dwellers both reflect this critique and offer the church a credible expression of faithful living that the wider culture can see and positively acknowledge. Take the example of the young woman unscrewing the arm rests on the park benches. When her story hit the media, many listeners would say 'that's an expression of Christianity I can agree with'.

Although edge communities were incredibly important to church renewal in history, they were numerically small compared to the size of the established church of the time. These edge expressions, which helped realign the wider Church to God's call, were not, and did not, become the main body. The church incorporated parts of what the pioneering communities were doing into the leadership and life of the wider church body. The prophetic communities were important as wayfinders, but for them to bring significant, holistic change, they needed to influence large swathes of the church. This is where we believe some recent movements labelled 'Emerging Church,' 'Fresh Expressions,' 'Alt-Church' and 'Missional Church' have been unhelpful in their claims. Typically, early on, the proponents of these movements made grand statements about being the future of the church. As if this new style of church would be THE expression of church rather than seeking to impact the wider centre-church.

What Centre-church offers

We cannot just sit back and watch the edge-dwelling entrepreneurs do their stuff. The centre has a crucial part to play in the renewal of the church. We have been formed in a certain church model and have risen to influential church positions because we are fluent in the culture and language of our church. That is a great gift for our churches but does not prepare us to intuitively bring necessary new shapes of mission. Whenever existing church leaders attempt to realign church and culture, we are fundamentally limited because we are trying to inhabit another cultural context (a second language) from our churched culture (our mother tongue).

Even if we study hard, read all the books and go to every seminar on post-post-modernity, globalisation and the rest, we will never fully understand. Take Alan, who has studied sociology – particularly that of Christian faith – to Ph.D. level, researching why people leave churches and what shapes their faith beyond church commitment. He has learnt a lot yet knows he does not naturally fit a community of people searching for truth, life and hope outside of the church. Like Alan, most church leaders do not have the time to gain fluency by immersing themselves in this new cultural context. They must keep the existing church going, working hard on the important core competencies of healthy church life.

Don't be discouraged by this reality. We are not alone; God works constantly to bring renewal and realign his church. We can have confidence that God is seeking to do this again in our time and culture.

Alan has been part of centre-church for 40 years, over 30 of those as a pastor in Baptist churches in New Zealand. He knows this space well and has seen how those at the centre of church life can be significant agents in renewal movements. This is a little of his story:

> In the 1970s I was a teenager in an Anglican church that was positively influenced by the charismatic movement. Our rapidly growing, charismatic youth group, often eclipsed the established adult congregation in numbers. I enjoyed the opportunities and experienced the generous inclusion given to us young charismatics by our wise vicar. He, and many of the wider church leadership, continually chose to embrace us teenagers, despite our overly enthusiastic, at times outrageous and dubious tendencies.
>
> Our Sunday night services were regularly a mix of a robed choir and a band of guitars played by bare-foot, long-haired, scruffy teenagers. The liturgy combined Old and New Testament readings with enthusiastic altar calls, opportunities for prayer for 'the baptism of the Holy Spirit' and emotional messages from youth leaders. Services followed the 1662 *Book of Common Prayer* and included

open prayer times calling on the Holy Spirit to heal, work miracles and give the ultimate gift of tongues.

When the service was over, it was off to the Vicar's place for supper, more worship, prayer and conversations around what God was doing. The vicarage was big, and the formal lounge could squash in over 50 young people all crammed on the floor or standing in doorways and perched on windowsills. Here was the centre-church embracing a new movement, giving us room to try, and opportunities to lead with consistent and wise support.

But that was only half of it. The Vicar's other work was validating, supporting and encouraging the many established congregants, furious about these crazy teenaged charismatics, who rightly complained our theology was more passion than exegetical reasoning. Our critics were wary of the open prayer times, Holy Spirit encounters and constant calls for conversion.

Looking back, the Vicar was both very patient and exceptionally wise. He allowed younger, competent leaders to lead the youth work but included us in the Sunday night services and hosted the Sunday evening suppers. He made room for, knew and supported us, but he didn't pretend he was part of us. At the same time, he visited congregation members who criticised what was happening, helped navigate the decisions of the vestry and ensured the Bishop heard the stories of young people coming to faith. He was intuitively playing the role of a centre-church leader in the in-tensional relationship we are describing.

The model of change we propose needs the interaction and combined strengths of centre-church leaders and apostolic edge-dwellers. We believe the Holy Spirit works through edge and centre together as they hold this in-tensional relationship with each other. Each needs its own space and role as they collaborate. If one thinks they can do it alone, or play the role of the other, they will fail.

Centre church has much to offer this in-tensional conversation and enormous strengths to draw on in reshaping the future. Centre churches are visible to the wider community in ways edge-communities can never be. Their building and signage are everywhere. They are recognised for community work, especially in times of personal crisis, and their work with the marginalised. Established churches can offer sought-after access to faith-based schooling, elderly care facilities, social housing etc. Communities turn to them for weddings or funerals, Christmas events or to send their children to youth group and the church buildings are often used by community groups.

Centre-churches have structures such as belonging to global denominations that give them credibility, inherited tradition, and institutional strength. They can seem broad, wise and safe. This institutional strength may have been undermined by sexual abuse offenses and links to colonising agendas but despite this, to varying degrees, the established church has credibility in the wider community. Centre-churches can also have enormous resources in property, access to money and infrastructure. For edge communities there are immediate opportunities in having connections with an established church. Being linked may provide understanding – 'oh you're part of St Tims' – and that brings some validation in the eyes of the community.

Centre-church offers safe places for faith exploration. You can enter a church and hide in the crowd, anonymous in a way you cannot be in small groups. Whereas an edge group may focus on a specific gospel charism, centre-church is broad, and holds many.

Strengths aside, we believe any realistic assessment of centre-church today would describe it as idolatrous and compromised. Accusations that call for significant realignment, change and new emphasis within our churches. As the dominant expression of the Christian faith, centre-churches need good leadership and sensitivity to new gospel life. In this time of flux, centre-church leaders and congregations need to focus on the core competencies of a thriving faith community, including: worship that reflects the congregation and has integrity with the church's realities; biblical preaching that speaks to people's needs; leadership serious about growing church health and life; inviting spaces and structures that lead to invitations into people's homes; pastoral care that helps people belong and can link in specialist care in a crisis; solid management, with financial and organisational systems and appropriate policies; a focus on children and youth that provides for age specific needs; a culture that fosters belonging; a sense of corporate identity; a desire for a caring Christ-like culture; life on life discipleship and a vision for a church that people can get behind.

These competencies may sound obvious, but they are critical to the life and growth of your church and therefore to the future of the church. If one or two of these competencies are poor, it hinders the whole church. It is necessary to constantly review, improve and strengthen each area.

The church must be rebuilt and realigned. Centre-church leaders focusing on core competencies help rebuild the church. Yet the Church must also be re-aligned to cultural needs and influenced by the incarnated alternatives of edge-church for real change to become reality. That is the tension.

The life cycle of Edge Communities

Edge-leaders and centre-church leaders should understand the typical life cycle of edge-communities. A new edge-community tends to be motivated and propelled by an 'against-energy;' an inherent angst triggered by a situation which lacks the Kingdom of God. It may be part of the wider society, for example, the needs of street people, a concern for struggling teenagers, refugees, or another marginalised group. Or it may be angst with centre-church, for example, the church's perceived complicity in the greed of modern consumerism in contrast to the gospel's call to simplicity and generosity. This anti energy gives edge-leaders and edge-communities a strong initial motivation and momentum. Their deconstruction of dominant values and lifestyles (whether centre-church or wider-society) propels them to live differently and create a radical alternative.

Against energy and motivating angst can spark an edge-community but it will not sustain it. The 'against' posture must transform into living a gospel focused alternative. This takes time, experimentation, and lots of prayer. To sustain their initiative, the early leaders need to find a group to journey with and together discern God's call for a new form of life. Core group relationships need to form and deepen, and the ability to live and work together must mature. This takes several years and a lot of energy, necessitating trials and refinements. Typically, the founding members attempt audacious, sometimes high-risk endeavours. These early ventures will be remembered, becoming the community's myths and legends, shaping who they are and what being part of their edge-community means.

This initial season is highly focused. Resources may be low, but the early leaders throw everything they have at growing their Kingdom expression. Their cause and community will be all consuming and the early years will feel draining, lonely, and risky. This is not the time for central-church engagement, nor for deep theological reflection, or developing best practice. This is a nose to the grindstone chapter. Everything will seem tenuous at this stage but these early beginnings, while fragile, are beautiful glimpses of the Kingdom of God expressed in community and the lives of those involved.

The beginning is demanding, exciting and invigorating and the next stage will inevitably feel mediocre. However, the transition from radical beginnings to routinisation is an essential step for the life and growth of the edge-community. Routinisation involves establishing procedures, processes, and guidelines that others can emulate, while perpetuating the vision and values. The edge-leadership will need to work on recruitment processes, how to prepare new leaders, decision making processes, establishing community rhythms, recording the community's ways of being, values and vision, structures, and forms of accountability. They must establish links with wider bodies to provide belonging, accountability, and conversation partners. Often leaders who excelled in the first stage struggle with routinisation and may need help. Allowing new people to come into the community may feel like a loss to early community members.

This is a maturing season that lays the foundations for the community, and the gospel work they have planted, to grow. Every process, procedure and way of making decisions needs to be debated and recorded. Lessons learnt must be formalized. The vision, values and rhythms of the community's life need to be embodied in enduring ways. In the beginning decision making may have been shared, organic and anarchic. Maybe the community sat down at night and argued or prayed a decision through. That was appropriate when the community was small but now leaders need to be named. Leadership processes and discernment/decision making guidelines must be documented so all community members, especially new ones, can see how the group operates.

The routinisation process helps the community to stay together, attract new members and bring through new leaders. Edge communities that struggled to become established may prefer to ignore or delay routinisation, but their sustainability and growth depends on it. This stage can be as demanding as the first. Some will argue that keeping a simple structure and leadership means remaining organic and responding quickly to new needs. They will say eschewing written documents, processes and procedures is advantageous, and more energizing for those involved. Unfortunately, it results in fragility and reduces the possibility of becoming a thriving, growing community over the long term.

The third season of an edge community's life cycle could be called the stage of influence. By now the edge-community has established positive gospel work designed to meet a specific need. It has faced difficulties, developed rhythms of life, systems of recruitment and attracted new people into community life. Leaders have been named and their roles articulated, leadership training and development steps are in place, necessary structures, procedures, and processes are available to all community members. At this point everyone knows the decision-making processes and is empowered to contribute.

In the Influence stage the edge-community can engage constructively with the wider church, sharing their gospel imperative and having positive impact. Justin writes of his experience: "It is helpfully humbling to Jenny and me to watch others, who have been influenced by our lives and conversations, doing a much better job of living these gospel imperatives than we ever have. Their lives and pioneering work are now calling us to return to true North and keep living a costly gospel lifestyle. By building communication and relationship with centre-church, we at the edge have found a much more holistic experience of what God is doing in and through his people. We have been given gifts and been able to share them within the body of Christ. We would have missed this had we stayed isolated from centre-church life."

Summary

❖ An In-tensional conversation between edge and centre church requires both parties to know what they are called to do, their strengths and weaknesses, and how they work best for gospel renewal.

❖ Edge-communities are living examples of a passionate and personally costly life following Jesus. This and their critique of the church (often mirroring the perspective of many in wider society whose voices are never heard by centre-church leaders) can be a gift in an In-tensional conversation with the centre.

❖ Centre-church is visible in the community, has longevity, local credibility, connections to wider denominational and other networks, relationships and resources, all of which they can bring to an In-tensional conversation with edge-leaders and their communities.

❖ Centre-churches are the future, and it is essential to keep working on the core competencies of a thriving church community, thus strengthening what Centre-church offer in an In-tensional relationship with the edge.

❖ The Edge-community life cycle involves three distinct stages. The radical days, followed by a necessary routinisation of the community life that leads to sustainability before it begins influencing centre-church and encouraging other edge-communities to begin.

Saying it again!

Let's reiterate: the edge communities of faith may be a small part of the future, but we see them as integral to the whole. The bulk of the future will be found in the centre-church, where society can most obviously and easily join into the body of Christ. Local congregations offer the beautiful depth and breadth of the Christian tradition in the sacred rituals of even the smallest Sunday service.

Our main points so far

❖ Western society is spiritually hungry; however, the church is not seen as wholly meeting this need.

❖ The Western Church is struggling with fruitfulness and faithfulness. We are in significant, potentially terminal, decline.

❖ The church must not fall into fatalism or triumphalism but embrace what it means to be a faithful people on a pilgrimage following Christ.

❖ The church is not called to be relevant but to offer a lived alternative to the deepest cultural angst of our times.

❖ The church needs to realign to God. We are struggling with idolatry and compromise; we are flabby and insipid.

❖ Existing centre-church leaders are not equipped to reinvent the church. They need to keep churches going, developing key competencies and building intentional relationship with edge-church.

❖ In each generation God raises up edge communities in response to the deep cultural needs of the time.

❖ Edge-communities have a common life cycle. If they create sustainable rhythms and pathways for new people and new leaders, they can become influential, having their prophetic voice widely heard and their apostolic approach copied.

❖ As the centre and edge relate, the centre can be renewed for another generation.

❖ We believe that through this In-tensional relationship, edge-communities can be supported, and centre-churches can sense new ways to live more gospel-centred, society-aligned expressions of Christian faith.

❖ The remainder of this book will bring the 'centre-edge' dialogue to life. We hope to help centre and edge see and understand how great they each are and just how much they need each other.

Chapter 6 — Radical

Centre and edge tend not to collaborate and may dismiss each other. We have been at too many pastors' meetings, church conferences and leadership gatherings where those working on the edge are viewed disparagingly. We have sat with edge-dwellers and know how they can judge and disparage centre-church leaders and established church life. We need to break down the stereotypes that separate us through In-tensional relationships of centre and edge leaders.

In the previous chapter we outlined the life cycle of edge communities through three distinct stages:

❖ Radical

❖ Sustainable

❖ Influential

In this chapter we will focus on the in-tensional conversation between centre and edge during the radical stage of an edge-community life cycle. Chapters seven and eight will focus on the sustainable and influential stages respectively. Understanding this life cycle will help both centre and edge leaders have realistic expectations of one another.

Both centre and edge need to accept this will always be a tense relationship. You will not inherently understand each other and will naturally have different priorities and approaches. Edge-dwellers, remember that even the most gracious centre-church congregations will struggle to accommodate you and the most generous and mature centre-leaders will find your presence challenging. Your ambivalence to church life will destabilise them and your critiques will be hard for them to hear – so be kind and gentle!

Centre-church leaders, understand that criticism from edge-leaders is a kinder version of what you would hear from the wider community outside the church. The edge is aware of people who long for spirituality and desire God but either feel alienated, or don't fit into centre-church life. Listening to this critique will prepare you for necessary conversations with those outside the church and those hurt by the church. Edge-dwellers are deeply in touch with society's cultural angst and personal pains. The edge are comfortable with change and can help centre leaders and congregations to develop an appetite for change.

Where our society is crying out for alternatives to the many crises we face, edge-dwellers are confident they have some real answers even when lived out in small, down-to-earth ways. Young edge-leaders know their generation's angst and desperately want to respond. Edge-dwellers love to try and find answers, giving it a crack with what they have and trusting God to fill in the gaps. Ballsy edge-dwellers often have the audacity to believe 'we can do this'. Their confidence and enthusiasm are a gift for the church in the west today.

If you are an edge-leader, eventually you'll need to commit fully to your call; to start something new, radical and tangible that speaks to societal angst and personal pain with the hope, faith and love of the gospel of Jesus. It means a lot of demanding work ahead and leaving behind some important things and ways of life. It's exciting and daunting. This new community of purpose will demand your full heart and attention for years to come.

While edge-leaders may have a powerful desire to deconstruct and critique the centre church, it is not OK to stand on the edge and criticise its failings. Edge-leaders need to focus on providing a tangible alternative and building something that shows a viable gospel initiative. Focus your reconstructive energy by making lasting, positive alternatives of Kingdom life. Reconstruction is harder than deconstruction, anyone can point out what is going wrong, but the vital prophetic gift is building viable hopeful alternatives. Staying true to your calling, focusing on your task and being gracious to others is a pathway to mature Christian leadership. Ironically, your influence grows when you walk this quiet path.

In the radical stage edge-leaders can work on their character by listening to criticism of their leadership style, being vulnerable enough to ask for more critique and humble enough to address what is raised. The neat thing about edge-communities is that they will bring your shadow sides to full visibility. That is a gift if you are self-aware enough to see the need to personally grow. Edge-leaders may need counselling, psychotherapy, spiritual direction and coaching from experienced leaders. We all come to leadership roles broken, messy and in need of renewal. This is the good news of the gospel for us as leaders as well as those we seek to serve.

Operating from Humility

Edge-leaders need to be confident, with a strong belief in their calling and what God is bringing to life through them and their team. They need a 'we can do this better' attitude. Over time this confidence needs to be tempered with humility, an awareness of the challenges and the inclusion of centre-church leaders.

As Justin says, "For edge-dwellers pride is a prevailing and challenging attitude that cannot be left unchecked. We as edge dwellers, need grace and humility if we are going to be effective in the Kingdom." The reality is God does not need any of us to do God's work. Our lives are all gift and being called into a segment of Kingdom work is a privilege. Pride, criticism, cynicism, and judgement shift us beyond a humble need for God and prevent the centre-church leaders from hearing our voices and seeing what we are building. No one appreciates an attitude of superiority. It repels others and is repellent to God.

Closer relationship with centre-church leaders is possible when edge-leaders foster a stance of humility, respect, and grace. Edge-leaders do not have all the answers, resources and leadership skills or a monopoly on God's calling, gifting, and power. Without God humbling edge-leader's pride their theology becomes ideology which cannot sustain them or their community or provide love to the people they serve. Humility helps develop resilience for the long haul. Edge-leaders and communities must not lose sight of their utter dependence on the Holy Spirit and all God wants to guide them into. We can remember too many edge communities who were genuinely engaging hurting people and concerns in prophetic ways but who lost the Holy Spirit's deep sustaining, and a humble connection with centre-church because of their self-aggrandisement and pride. Edge-leaders need to develop a level of humility and respect for others to protect the life of their communities from a toxicity of pride, arrogance and even bitterness. That is tough to write and even sadder to have observed.

Forming a team that becomes an enduring community focused on a particular gospel expression is both hard and essential. Offering the wider community and centre-church a glimpse of where God is at work in the shared life of a community is more compelling than the voice of lone leader. Centre-leaders have seen charismatic leaders come and go. Often, they start something that looks promising but is dependent on their strengths and gifts and when they lose interest or energy or feel called elsewhere then everything they started falls away. The shared life of an intentional community that is multipliable, transferable, and accessible for others is a wonderful invitation for centre-church to consider.

Edge-leaders, you need to acknowledge the limits of capacity and look for ways to simplify the lives of the people in your edge-community. Where you can, try and let things count twice. This might mean that when we volunteer to help at a church BBQ, we also invite along a neighbour we want to spend time with. Or when we are asked to bless someone's house in our neighbourhood, we invite someone from the church to come with us. We need to ask this question: how can we do what we are doing in a way that blesses or influences the wider church and how can we offer our gifts without over-committing or withdrawing from our primary calling?

We need to find invitational steps so that others can see what we do, experience the dynamic of Kingdom life we are part of and be offered steps toward supportive formation. This allows people to take entry level steps alongside those who have been on the path for a long time. Neglecting new recruits is damaging to them, to the movement and to the relationship with the centre church.

In the radical stage establish your community and gospel expression well, so as you enter the sustainable stage you are better prepared for greater discipleship and multiplying. It is helpful to develop structures for the worst-case scenario rather than for an unrealistic team made up of perfect people. Doing so ensures you and your community are ready for when things go wrong, and it lays a foundation for the next stage.

Centre-church

Understanding the typical life cycle of edge-communities will help you know how to approach edge-leaders at each stage, understanding what they may need from you and seeing what they may be able to offer you and your congregation.

Often the person gifted with a calling to address a particular societal angst starts as part of centre-church. These potential edge-leaders choose to leave centre-church altogether (or are encouraged to leave) because they do not fit centre-church life, services, and structures. When this happens both centre-church and the new mission groups suffer. Often one or both are seriously damaged or end up closing. To be most effective they need an In-tensional relationship that gives each space but allows connection. They can recognise each-other's role and calling, making room for each other, and allowing each to be self-governing. Their In-tensional connection and communication mean they learn from the other and are supported and inspired through the other's stories and life.

Centre-leaders should not try to tame mission initiatives and leaders by enticing or forcing them to fit into centre-church structures and life. Sadly, a common pattern in New Zealand churches over the last few decades has seen people with new gospel initiatives and leadership potential tamed into centre-church roles, paid employment in the church or encouraged to stay within rather than venturing out after a new gospel venture. Centre-church leaders have an obligation to look for and listen to those on the edge of our churches and intentionally build respectful relationship with them that encourage and support them in their edge-community calling.

Church-leaders may be tempted to pay edge-leaders but we caution against offering money too soon. Going unpaid reduces expectations on the edge-leader, ensures their freedom and frees you from accounting for where church money is spent. It removes any demand for results. Another, more important reason is that when you start being paid it shifts your sense of dependency. When you feel called by God into a new venture, being dependent on God's provision draws you much deeper into what God is opening. At the stage when a radical gospel expression is emerging history tells us that these renewal movements are best left as lay-movements outside the financial support and potential entanglement of centre-church. Not paying an edge-leader does not mean centre-leaders cannot be financially supportive. There may be other ways the centre-church can encourage with financial support.

Centre-church leaders can support edge-leaders by backing them as people: Have confidence in them, listen to their calling and pray for and with them. You need to be discerning and wise to identify potential edge-leaders. Many prophetic leaders are rough around the edges and do not fit our understanding of a church leader So how do you discern a potentially prophetic leader from a crazy idealist?

Here are a few clues:

❖ Edge-leaders will have a mission focus. They want to see people, especially those they feel distinctly called to coming to faith in Jesus and they are passionately committed to this happening.

❖ Look for evidence of a constructive life-giving gospel vision that others want to be part of.

❖ Leaders have followers. A prophetic or apostolic leader will attract at least a few others who want to get behind them.

❖ Leaders grow teams, attracting people and growing them in faith in Jesus and their commitment to each other.

❖ Edge-leaders develop the faith of the people who join them and the people they feel called to serve.

❖ There is evidence of Kingdom shaped discipleship.

As you prayerfully discern whether a potential leader is someone you could encourage and support, watch what they are building and their followers. Offer small encouragements and supports while you get to know them and grow your confidence in them. You will not always get it right, and that is part of finding edge-leaders to form In-tensional relationships with. Do not be put off if a potential edge-leader seems immature or an extreme personality. They have much to learn along the way. Often edge-leaders are not only entrepreneurial and challengingly prophetic but also messy, chaotic, and self-confident. If they are arrogant and critical of centre-church and centre-leaders, being round them will be painful. Getting to know each other will soften critique and grow trust. This is the foundation of an In-tensional relationship, which benefits both centre and edge and will form the church of tomorrow.

Edge-leaders have an against energy. That means they need something to push away from. Edge-church people push away from centre-church. Their critical, anti-authority, anti-institution, deconstructive energy is difficult when they critique the work you lead and feel called to. Forming In-tensional relationships with edge-leaders requires centre-church leaders to be grounded in their own calling and unphased by the critique.

Alan has heard the critiques of many edge-leaders, watched their gospel initiatives and seen the people they attract and the communities they develop. In his experience it is almost always uncomfortable to listen to edge-leaders dismiss centre-church. They want change and they want it now. Alan says, "on reflection, spending time with edge-leaders and edge-communities have been some of the most hopeful and lifegiving times of my three decades as a centre-church leader". Alan reminds himself that it is okay that he doesn't understand them, or the way they operate; they could be the very people who develop a community that sparks new structures, vision and renewal across the church.

In this in-tensional conversation centre-church leaders need to be acutely aware of their calling and their part to play. Acknowledge that centre-church is incomplete without the edge-communities and edge-life. Centre-church leaders are not well positioned to change the structures, services, and systems they lead, work and worship within. But edge-leaders understand the subtle cultural language and deep concerns and cultural biases of those in wider secular society. Centre-church leaders need to develop a posture of leaning out towards and in support of the edge-dwellers. Leaning out demands a repeated and intentional posture of connecting with and supporting potential edge-leaders. The centre may understand the theory of post-modernism, secular culture or a specific subculture, that doesn't make us fluent inhabitants of that culture. The services and mission initiatives the centre-church creates won't naturally connect with people beyond the church.

The centre's role is not to lead and shape the new gospel initiatives, but to support and authenticate the emerging leaders and movements. This means putting our mana (respect and backing) behind them. We may have questions and concerns, but our role is to guard these leaders and create space for them to develop their new initiatives. In this way we protect their capacity and focus, removing expectations on them to be strongly involved in centre-church activities or weighed down by the centre's criticisms and concerns. God renews the church through raising up edge-dwellers within our midst. When the edge can commit to long-term effective mission, it will influence the wider society and help bring health to centre-church as well.

Edge-dwellers will demand complete commitment from themselves and their team and will possibly not see or credit the commitments of centre-church leaders. They will not see that many centre-church attenders have limited capacity and demanding commitments elsewhere. They will see centre-church as safe and stable but lacking commitment and a heart for change. They will critique centre-church as risk-averse and limiting the work of God. Support them anyway.

As centre-church leaders get alongside edge-leaders they may want to introduce them to the congregation and involve them in church life but edge-dwellers in the radical stage just need to get on with their own calling. Helping them keep this focus is the best support you can offer. Keep the new venture quiet at this stage and give the edge-dwellers time to develop, to make mistakes without an audience and to find their way. As a rough guide we'd suggest that you help them stay out of the limelight for at least two years.

Expect new edge-leaders to fail and make mistakes. Innovating results in more false starts and complex challenges than following a proven formula. Our role is to help them learn from failures and challenges as these lessons will refine and re-shape the gospel expression they are co-creating with God. Many of the lessons will be personal. To lead well they will need to face their own insecurities and baggage, which demands a courageous willingness for deep self-reflection.

Of all the reasons people don't stick in new gospel ventures, one stands out. It is easier to walk away than honestly face one's own character issues, and courageously work through them. Someone with leadership potential becomes a leader out of the struggle of dealing with their weaknesses, failures, and blind spots. Good mentoring can help the edge-leaders assess how they and their team are doing and progressing. Structural critiques are best held back during the radical phase, as the focus should be on getting something up and running.

Summary

During the radical stage of an edge-community's life cycle an intensional relationship between centre and edge leaders can emerge if they meet and choose to see the best in each other.

❖ Centre-church leaders will often need to take the initiative in forming a relationship with an edge-leader and to carefully discern potential edge-leaders from wild cards.

❖ The edge must focus on building the new gospel expression they feel called to.

❖ Centre-leaders need to build the centre-church and let edge-dwellers lead the new gospel venture.

❖ Team development or community formation will take much of the edge-leader's time and energy.

❖ Personal character issues will arise for edge-leaders as they move deeper into the new gospel venture and edge-community formation. Working on these issues is essential; centre-leaders can encourage and support this work.

❖ Centre leaders should not rush to pay edge leaders but support them personally: buy them a coffee, help them find good resources, send them to a useful course, book them a weekend away.

Chapter 7 — Sustainable

What the Edge does

Moving from a radical start-up to a sustainable and long-term gospel expression is a shift in focus for edge-leaders and communities. The longer a community expresses a gospel lifestyle, the more convincing and hopeful it becomes to those the edge-community seeks to reach; to edge-community members themselves; to observers who see a new thing emerging; to centre-church leaders and congregations. These gospel expressions can become sustainable and deepen connections into the community, broadening their influence over time.

A sustained response requires maintaining positive long-term relationships with the people we seek to connect with. It takes time to build trust, offer and receive belonging and see transformation through relationships. Too often Christians turn up offering great things and then leave, destroying the hope and trust they had in the people group they sought to serve. Working toward a sustained response gives edge-communities a growing influence at a more systemic level of transformation.

A stable edge-community is positive not only for those we seek to support but also for our own children and family life. It is beneficial for our children to have longer seasons where we consolidate, allowing them to have roots and belonging in a stable community life. It is a powerful, shaping experience for children to grow up seeing their parents modelling a long-haul missional commitment, through sustained prayer, personal cost and dedication.

Communities become sustainable through a thorough process of routinisation. The structures and systems developed through routinisation enables ordinary edge-community members to be outstanding. It allows others to catch the vision, sync into the community and become leaders in the movement. When new leaders can understand the values of the shared life, the edge-community can grow and multiply. Having outlined some of the gains of moving into the sustainable stage let's look at some of the common elements of this routinisation process.

A crucial aspect of the routinisation process is articulating clear formational pathways for new people to join the community, be mentored, and supported so they can grow into leadership. Naming what people need to know and understand about this community and its life, the expectations for new people joining the community, and the support the community will offer them. Rather than relying on new people just learning by osmosis, when edge communities work on routinisation there is greater safety and clarity for newcomers.

Some of the people you attract will be part of centre-church. The possibility of them joining your edge-community life needs to be carefully negotiated with centre-church leaders who may feel strongly about 'good people' being recruited by you. The centre-church leaders need to see the Kingdom benefit of people being involved in an edge-community, for their discipleship and the longer-term positive impact on the church. We all, centre-church leaders and edge community leaders, need to remember the people who work with us are people we are called to care for, disciple and encourage. They are not ours! They are God's! There is something deeply wrong when leaders, centre or edge, consider people as theirs.

In the sustainable phase edge-communities need to identify and name a rhythm of life, making commitments to rhythms of prayer, rest, and reflection. This means naming and sustaining regular community prayer times and making room for personal prayer and reflection. It means creating expectations of rest and recreation and ensuring times of community fun, relaxing meals and shared moments of life together. This will entail a shift from the organic ways of the radical start-up. It may feel like structures, rules and processes are taking over, but naming shared rhythms can bring immense freedom and health for all. The rhythms offer a formation process for new people, ways for leaders to develop, and help to prevent individual burnout. Keeping a weekly Sabbath, annual holidays and an expectation of personal seasonal sabbaticals all help shape and hold edge-communities and their people over the long term.

Edge-communities need to consciously focus on bringing in new people of different ages and stages. Recognising that different age groups bring different gifts to community life. Older people may have less energy and more commitments to children, ageing parents, or grandchildren than young single adults, but they also bring life experience, wisdom, and perhaps a slower pace and a longer-term perspective. Young adults typically bring high energy and engagement, but they also need more community times, shared fun, personal mentoring, and more stretching opportunities than older people. Couples with children or people who have been in the community for many years also bring strengths to your community life but may not have the same available time or energy as others. The community rhythms you create in this stage must align with the initial call to activism, engagement, hospitality and discipleship but they can also be tailored to the differing capacities and needs of community members. Finding ways to incorporate these differing needs and encouraging differing roles within community life is all part of routinisation.

A significant part of the routinisation process is clarifying who leads and how leadership functions within this edge-community. From our experience, in Aotearoa, this is often fraught. We live in a time in history where severe critiques of leadership are common and in the worst situations the critics can become abusive. When a radical edge expression begins it will be small, so issues of leadership are not always necessary to clarify. Leaders just emerge and typically the focus on the goal means all leadership strength is welcomed. But quickly, as more people join, the questions of how leadership functions and how is leadership chosen will need to be resolved. Leadership needs to be seen as a gift that resources and enables the whole edge-community. The edge-community should mandate and release leaders to lead in ways that are clear, and understood by all. It is worthwhile spending time together discussing and formulating answers to questions like:

❖ How does leadership look on the worst day, when the edge community is teetering on the brink of falling apart? It is easy to imagine a good day but naming how we will operate when things are at their worst helps bring security and clear paths for tough seasons.

❖ What do we mandate leaders to do, and how do we expect them to lead? When do they need to come back to the whole edge-community to discuss the way forward together?

❖ If the community can't find agreement on a decision – how will we decide? How will we include (or exclude), and look after those who disagree with a decision made by our agreed process?

Part of growing sustainability is clarifying safety mechanisms. Answering the questions above together and documenting how we will behave and make decisions when things are tough strengthens everyone and the shared community.

No-one expects there to be complaints, disagreements and even accusations of abuse in their community, but; if people have a problem with the recognised leadership that they feel they cannot resolve by talking to the leader; then where can they go to for help? In the early days of the life of the edge-community the founders have an implicit mandate to lead. But now as the edge-community becomes more sustainable and new people are joining, leaders and the leadership process, including where to go for help when there are serious concerns, need to be clarified. This challenge is even greater when the founder moves out of leadership in the community or leaves the community altogether. Then the new leaders and the community members need clarity on how to move forward.

All communities need leadership. It is a primary role that somebody or somebodies must do. It is safer to have that leadership clearly named with appropriate processes than pretend no-one leads, or we are all leading this community together. There is another whole book needed on the leadership dynamics of edge-communities but for now just a few thoughts based on where we have seen edge communities get out of balance.

Firstly, there is a tension between the apostolic and pastoral needs in every community and this tension needs to be carefully navigated. People have real needs and need to be cared for, but the momentum and prophetic edge of the community must be maintained. Pastoral leaders often lose direction and energy and don't appreciate the need to keep pushing forward even when the pace feels uncomfortable to some. Apostolically wired leaders need to remember to take people with them; others are not pawns in a Kingdom venture.

Secondly, leaders need to make sure that the structures and rhythms of the edge community are sustaining life in the edge-community and sustainable in a way that is not excessively demanding or draining. Someone, it may not be the leader, needs to be monitoring the structures and rhythms to ensure they are nurturing life and ensuring the health of community members and the community as a whole. Someone who is close to the apostolic leader and who can work well with them should be delegated for this role.

Finally, leaders need to be role models. If they are calling others to a high-cost lifestyle for the Kingdom, then they must model the highest price commitment in their own lives. They need to ensure this lifestyle is sustainable for them and those they are calling to follow them. Crucially, edge leaders need to be developing personal and faith resilience so they can remain a non-anxious presence if it all goes to custard.

In summary, leaders need to have a long-term commitment, intuitively navigate the edge charism and culture and be constantly working on their own character.

Ironically as edge-communities mature they need to create spaces for differing levels of commitment. This is probably a massive shift from the start-up days when it was expected that everyone was 100%, if not 120% committed. Now the culture and understanding of the community members must shift to allow for the long term fully-committed, those just popping in to see if it's the space for them and everything in between. For example, Urban Vision have created an intentional three-year formation process.

With clear spaces for people to have different commitments and involvement in the edge-community life, it is necessary to consider how that impacts on decision making. When people have differing levels of commitment to community life and the community's longevity then their respective input in decision making needs to be clarified. Everybody's voice can be heard but there should be mechanisms that ensure the voices of the long-term, committed people carry more weight. These people have to live with the consequences of decisions differently to those who have just joined, have a smaller commitment and investment, or could be leaving soon.

As the edge-community develops greater sustainability and incorporates new people with differing levels of involvement and commitment it must protect against losing its mission focus, discipleship edge and what we have called white-hot faith. The edge needs to create mechanisms to address missional drift.

Encouraging new cycles of critique, discernment and renewal within the edge community as a regular practice keeps the vision current and the gospel expression sharp. What was cutting edge a few years ago can quickly become compromised, miss a key gospel imperative or societal need, and lose its prophetic thrust. Reviewing the community's life and work can inspire reform and refresh the pioneers, allowing for new life.

Edge-leaders must grasp that cycles of radical pioneering are often followed by a focus on establishing clear rhythms, roles and patterns that will sustain prophetic communities. Edge movements cycle through predictable phases of radical start-up, becoming sustainable and having influence as they become more visible and accessible to the wider church. These changes in community needs mean leaders must be able to change gear in their leadership style, expectations and mode.

Changing Gear

Edge-leaders may not enjoy the suggestion that they move into a management phase. Leaders who are entrepreneurial enough to start a new edge-community, typically despise management. To them the routinisation steps we have described will feel like compromise or a waste of time. However, to grow the community they need to develop classic management and systems skills. It's not entertaining work, but there are a couple of short cuts. Historically lots of groups simply copied others. Dominic, for example, took the rule of St Augustine off the shelf and applied it in his community. People with organising skills can be brought in to help write down what entrepreneurial leaders know but never quite have time to document. If you do bring skilled people in to document your community's patterns and life, edge-leaders need to carefully guide this process so that the vision, DNA, charism and heartbeat of the community and its work is not lost.

The process of routinisation names a particular edge communities' vision, values and operations, and tells its story. Routinisation develops practices that others can lead and facilitate to continue the community's work. This allows new leaders to take on key tasks and allows for 'ordinary', hardworking, caring leaders to thrive without needing to be prophetic or pioneering. A thorough process of routinisation strengthens the community and releases the pioneers to mentor others and focus on new ventures. Setting up systems and structures does not mean losing your heart and white-hot faith commitments. Keeping the King, Jesus Christ central to your Kingdom work is the pearl of great price and holding that pearl tightly will ensure you don't simply become a very good social service agency without charism and key purpose.

Without routinising, edge movements will likely rely on the leadership of one or two charismatic personalities, leading powerfully through their apostolic and prophetic gifting, to hold the group together. Such passionate leadership inspires communities and, with healthy accountability, can become a credible influence in the wider church, however reliance on only one or two strong founding voices is risky. For longevity's sake edge-communities need to move into a phase where leadership is named, more widely distributed and other leaders raised up.

The relationship between the Edge's needs and the Centre-church

With the sustainability phase, another gear change is needed in the connections with centre-church. Edge-leaders should focus on building a bridge with centre-church to strengthen the gospel expression and allow people they are helping to explore faith in Jesus and integrate into a place of broader engagement and support. George Ling draws on Ralph Winter's work saying – "Winter's thinking urges even the pioneers (*edge-leaders*) to change their minds. They need to think as deeply and passionately about the Church as they do about mission. One core element of historic sodal (*centre*) church, which is seen in Paul, Benedict, Francis, Ignatius etc is that they love the church, because Christ does, while working for her to become what she should be and is currently failing to live out. Some who have studied the role of founders insist this love is what makes them valued founders, not just noisy rebels."[14]

Routinisation is a maturing process that involves recognising the edge is not the complete answer. Rather it needs whole body of Christ. Humility for an edge-leader is knowing not everyone can or should live out the gospel as edge-dwellers. While edge-leaders and edge-communities can be prophetic and revitalising, they are not everything and they are not for everyone. They embody a distinct calling to be treasured and respected but there are many other important gospel works to be done within centre-church structures and congregations.

For some people who come to faith through edge communities, life is already stressful and joining the rhythms of a highly committed, apostolic edge-community can be too demanding or just inappropriate. They may need a season in a centre-church community where there is space to sit and receive for a while. It is exciting to see friends in our neighbourhoods come to faith and join some aspects of edge-community life, but not all can commit to the same level of involvement as the edge-members. They may not yet be free enough from an addiction or a difficult background to be able to make the kinds of commitments required of edge-communities. Being part of the wider church brings them necessary life and acceptance. Forming a trusting relationship with a centre-church that understands your edge-community's work and vision can provide the support your friends will need.

Likewise, some of our edge-people's capacity or health may change over time and they may need a season away from the stresses of the edge. Within Urban Vision Communities some people have had children with complex health needs or have parents or partners who have suffered life crushing events and needed greater care. Moving into a less demanding, more structured centre-church expression of faith has been nurturing and life-giving for these people. They remain part of the Urban Vision family and community while living outside of the high commitment communities.

There may be support for families of edge communities in linking their children into a centre-church children's programme or a youth group. Typically, there are not sufficient teenagers in an edge-community to form their own youth group and joining the local church youth group provides a peer group and time away from Mum and Dad's expression of faith. Children of edge-leaders may need time in the mainstream church to find their own faith at a healthy distance from their parents. Space, and careful mentoring from people outside of their parent's circles, allows them to do their own deconstruction. It is important that teenagers who need to push against their edge-community have a supportive alternative in the centre church.

Giving people freedom to move from centre-church to edge-church and sometimes back again is healthy for individuals and strengthens both centre and edge. Developing a strong bridge of respect between the two, perhaps sharing worship times or ministry, is crucial to building and maintaining a life-giving relationship. A bridge necessitates a closeness between the two communities that allows people from both sides to know one another and support each other's work. This enables people who are moving out of an edge community, or reducing their commitment for a season, to be nurtured by wider church life.

Where the edge cannot meet someone's needs, the local centre-church probably can. While edge-leaders may want to dissuade people from a consumeristic lifestyle that's rarely challenged in centre-church, we don't want to dissuade people from belonging to the body of Christ. Edge-leaders will struggle to find willing people of faith to support their mission dreams if they can't enter a local church and begin respectful conversations and join worship and events. Justin would go further, recommending that every edge-group sit at the back of a local church somewhere. If their new gospel expression is in the form of a church plant, then find another regular way of connecting with a wider group of Christians and centre-leaders.

By forming strong connections with centre-church leaders and congregations, edge-communities can intentionally offer ways for people in the centre-church to hear a calling to a radical lifestyle and to come and join them. Giving people opportunities to dip their toes into edge realities and move out of their comfort zone, is part of the edge-communities' calling within the body of Christ. Doing this with the knowledge and support of the centre-church leadership demands a strong edge-centre relationship.

Centre-church and edge-dwellers often don't hear each other well. The lived realities and key voices that shape their world views are fundamentally different; they may feel they are speaking different languages. That is why we call this an In-tensional relationship. Both centre-church and edge-church need to anticipate misunderstandings and misconceptions. Edge-dwellers need do their best to explain carefully and graciously, acknowledging that their focus is a narrow one, while the centre tends towards a broader view of things. A healthy edge-centre relationship requires significant work in the sustainability stage of an edge-community's life cycle. This relationship becomes more significant in the influential stage.

The key difficulty in developing this relationship often lies in the edge-dweller's provocative and uncomfortable message. Edge-leaders, you have the responsibility to help centre-church people see what you see. You don't need to compromise the message, but you do need to humbly communicate gospel challenges without causing unnecessary offense. Allow time to welcome centre-church people into your lives and communities. What you are doing is often best understood when witnessed, rather than explained from a distance. Many centre-leaders will need several visits and ask many questions before they have confidence to talk to their congregations about your work.

When communicating with centre-leaders and congregations, edge-leaders must carefully consider who is listening, seeking healthy commonalities and prayerfully discerning which part of the gospel challenge to highlight. It requires wisdom, and disciplined discernment about what to say to whom and when. It is loving to hold back on our provocation and challenge, respectfully helping others take it one step at a time. This might mean going over the basics of a missional call even while we're eager to share about more complex development or community ideas. Keep it simple at first, you will lose listeners by diving too deep too soon.

Justin and Jenny have lived these In-tensional relationships. They know the constant tension with the centre and have run into trouble by blurting out too many challenging thoughts regarding centre-church life. Justin says, "we came to realize this was unhelpful to others and to us. But most importantly it didn't help either edge communities or the centre-church to grow in gospel influence or in relationship together". When Justin and Jenny changed church community, they wanted to try a different approach and decided to stop telling people what they thought. They made a personal commitment not to share their thoughts about controversial topics – especially regarding the shape or focus of centre-church – without an agreement on how the conversation would flow first. As a result, they became more disciplined in what they contributed, timelier in their comments and easier to have around. They found they enjoyed being around centre-church leaders, structures and people more. The greatest gain was being taken very seriously when they did contribute to the conversation.

Some edge-dwellers will hear this as compromise. Yet if we look to the past, we see that all pioneering apostolic communities have lived in this tension. Every new apostolic movement that has positively influenced change in the wider church has been led by leaders who have tempered their critiques, developed trust and played the long game, helping centre-church leaders learn at their own pace.

Justin remembers when he and Jenny wanted to move to more part-time work and were advised against it by their wise and committed pastor who was conscious of their financial future. This well-meant advice cut across their sense of God's call. Justin also recalls when they wanted to buy land to pioneer a contemporary monastery of prayer and hospitality and were reluctantly supported by church leaders who couldn't see a future given the limited resources they had. Their fear was reasonable, but the endeavour succeeded. While understandable, these moments were disheartening for Justin and Jenny. Accepting the risk-averse centre moves slowly and holds conventionally wise views that can be contrary to edge-dweller's values can be deeply painful. It takes a depth of humility on behalf of edge-dwellers.

Edge-leaders will become frustrated when they notice missed opportunities and the layers of bureaucracy centre-church must negotiate every time they try new things. For Jenny and Justin this has become a tension within their marriage. As Bishop, Justin often sides with the centre-leaders and structures, whereas Jenny experiences Anglican meetings from her edge position, afterwards confidently listing all the things the church should do immediately. 'You really have no idea what it's like', has become a common and mutually frustrating mantra in their marriage. Jenny can't bear how slow-moving an old institutional church can be. She sees the obvious opportunities and needs, the gospel imperatives and untapped resources. As part of the centre-church leadership, Justin has come to learn it is a slow burn approach rather than a pioneering fire. However, once the fire is lit in centre-church, it is unlikely to burn itself out.

Edge-dwellers need to remember that centre-church leaders focus on and prioritise things that the edge find unimportant and irrelevant. When edge-leaders challenge this, centre-church leaders will feel threatened and offended. Centre-church leaders are generalists, and they do many things. Like medical doctors in general practice, they have an array of different roles and work needs. Edge-dwellers are like specialists who do far fewer things far more deeply.

The sustainability phase opens new areas of learning for edge-leaders, which are often encountered through painful connection with centre-church. At this point, committing to read widely can help you grow as a leader. Others have navigated this stage of becoming sustainable and their stories can encourage you when the going is tough. Form relationships with others leading similar intentional gospel communities. These people understand you, and being with them is deeply encouraging. Being with your tribe for events, workshops, gatherings and sharing good coffee is deeply restoring and inspiring. Learn from other's stories and where possible, copy the things that have worked well.

It is so important that followers of Jesus, particularly those in positions of influence, are determinedly committed to maturing their own character. The stakes of remaining immature and insecure are too high. If we agree that edge-communities can be, and should be, influential, then this challenge certainly applies to their leaders. Edge-leaders must choose between being influential for the Kingdom of God or being influential against it. It is that simple. If edge-leaders become a negative advert for the lifestyle they are calling people into, their prophetic voice becomes blunt or, worse still, a damaging influence.

Too often edge communities are known for the arrogant way they smash and bash the centre-church from a perceived sense of superiority. While the angry, cynical approach is easy to adopt, it is exceptionally destructive to positive influence and change within centre-church leaders and communities. Constructive in-tensional dialogue demands a maturity of character in edge-leaders, evidenced by humility, vulnerability and a willingness to listen. Unrestrained ego, personal insecurity and immaturity can draw edge-leaders to seeing themselves as superior to the leaders and people of centre-church. This unhelpful stance does not glorify God.

The relationship with centre-church is not the only site of potential damage. Unfortunately, edge-leaders are known for speaking detrimentally about other edge communities. This is often born out of personal insecurity, an unwarranted sense of superiority or in an ugly spirit of competition. Recently Justin and Jenny hosted a leader who had led an amazingly radical community in some of the poorest neighbourhoods in the world. When he was called into another season of ministry, he used his new platform to publicly criticize his previous community: explaining why it wasn't good at the things he was now committed to. Reflecting on this, Justin says he found it damaging to this leader's credibility that he publicly knocked the community he was part of for so long. It undermined both the ongoing work of that community, and his own prophetic voice. The man's message was something the wider church needed to hear, but it was lost because his hurtful, unwise comments made it easy for people to dismiss him.

Both Alan and Justin know from experience, that there is a tendency among edge-groups to put others down, to rejoice in other's weaknesses and to claim, 'we are more radical than another gospel expression'. Such talk is anti-gospel and toxic. We are called to build each other up, learn from each other and share resources. If what others are doing is exhibiting the Kingdom of God, we must endorse and encourage it and those giving their lives in obedience to Jesus. We must each find the internal grounding, inner peace and personal stability to live fully into our calling with faithfulness and integrity. This enables our voice to be heard by other edge-leaders and communities and the wider church.

Finally, edge communities and leaders need to be aware that insecurities and the ego's drive to succeed can lead to unhealthy and unbalanced lives. To show the gospel influence of edge-communities for the long haul, we must work on our personal baggage and vulnerabilities while supporting each other to live well. We will never find our worth, belonging, identity or sense of self-esteem in what we do. We need to diligently nurture our prayerful foundation, glorifying God and practising gratitude. Otherwise, we risk modelling a life that is both unhealthy for us and unreachable by others. We owe it to God to work on our personal wholeness, ensuring we are functioning from our gifts and calling rather than from a need to compensate our pain and brokenness. Humility, grace, integrity, authenticity, vulnerability, care, tenacity and respect are the true marks of character we need to leak out of our movements.

What the Centre does

For a centre-church leader to form an in-tensional relationship with an edge-community you must find one to connect with. You may already have some sustainable edge-communities or edge-ventures around your church or denomination. There may be local ones you don't yet know about, and you may need to find people to help you unearth them. When you do locate an edge-community, begin with a cup of coffee with one of the key members. No expectations and no promises. Ask for an opportunity to see what they are doing and to meet other community members. Let them know about your church and the church's heart for mission. Make sure you are not the only link person, take another member of the centre-church leadership with you to meet the edge-dwellers and discuss how the church may be able to connect. Over many months a relationship may form where you and the church you lead can help the edge-community to grow.

Now that the edge-community is past the first radical stage and they are consolidating through developing processes, systems and rhythms, new leaders, and pathways for newcomers, the relationship with the centre can be more intentional.

At this stage financial support and advice from the centre can be helpful. Once edge-leaders have proven themselves, they may need resources: to help purchase property, to provide administration support, or to pay part of a salary. Most of the work will be voluntary and most of the money will come from the community itself, but the centre's help can be encouraging and help build sustainability. The centre-church may connect the edge with people who have legal or financial expertise, or who may be willing to donate from their wealth or business to an exciting gospel venture.

Another support centre-churches may offer at this time is helping to frame a sustainability grid or giving advice around systems and processes. Somewhere in the centre-church's history will be relevant key learnings and resources, and a key person with specialist knowledge. In this season it's critical for the centre-church to present all the sustainability resources and people like building blocks and allow the edge community to assemble them in new and creative ways. The centre must step up in the sustainability season, but as a servant, saying: 'All this is available to you; tell us what you want and how you want to put it together'.

Start to tell the stories of the edge-community to your church or at wider church and denomination meetings. Giving them a platform to share their stories can be encouraging for everyone involved. Their story is one of the things that God is doing in your wider community. Keep the focus on what God is teaching them. You help keep these edge-communities safe by not exposing them too much.

Summary

- ❖ For an edge community to continue to grow, be sustainable and potentially multiply and continue long enough to be influential; it will need to actively work at naming and developing structures, rhythms and process that produce sustainability.

- ❖ Routinisation may be unattractive to the founders and early adopters who loved the early 'loose' days of the edge-communities life. However, to sustain community life beyond the commitment, giving attention to maintaining structures, leadership processes, prayer and community rhythms, formation and discipleship, is vital.

- ❖ The edge-community needs to develop good processes of recruitment and formation, as well as rules and rhythms of life.

- ❖ The community will need to adjust for members of different ages and stages of life, balancing inclusion with ensuring the unique charism and life of the community is not diluted or lost.

- ❖ Leaders, what they lead and how, needs to be addressed and clarified.

- ❖ The edge-community needs to reflect constantly on how it can continue to learn and not stagnate as it takes on rhythms and processes for sustainability.

- ❖ The edge-community needs to develop good administration and management systems which undergird the continued growth and strength of the community's gospel expression.

❖ In this routinisation season, edge-leaders and communities realise that they need the centre church, because:

- Edge-communities can learn from the centre-church.

- Edge-communities need good on and off ramps giving healthy flow between the edge-community and the centre-church.

- Edge-communities might be ready for some resourcing help from the centre.

❖ Finally, the Edge-community leaders need to work hard on their character. As things develop and grow the maturity of the edge-communities and their leader's character will become the prime limiting factor for future growth and influence.

Chapter 8 — Influential

What the Edge does

If you are an edge-leader whose community and mission are best described as influential, then you probably didn't need to read this chapter. You already know it. Of course, we'd love you to read on and compare your story with our thoughts. But we'd also love your input, because this book is intended to amplify your voice. Our email addresses are at the back of the book. Please get in touch.

Once your edge-community is established and routinised with stable and enduring systems for recruitment, formation, leadership development and ways for both the highly committed, and those of lesser capacity to contribute, you are well on the road to growing your influence. The influence you have in the lives of the people you seek to care for and in the wider church will be growing. Hopefully centre-church leaders have come alongside you to form in-tensional relationships and conversations in which they can learn from you and be inspired by the work you do.

Your next piece of work is ensuring multiplication. This begins through strengthening your leadership. Perhaps an external advisory group, comprised of people outside your community, would help. These groups are like a ship's keel; often unseen but whose presence brings wisdom, depth and a stabilising influence to your edge-community. As the community grows, so too does the demand on leadership. At this stage you need a 'leader of leaders', requiring different skills to the kind of leader needed at the previous stages. This person is leading peers through character development, collaboration, establishing outcomes and qualities of leadership and then holding everyone, including themselves, accountable. If this isn't you, then you have a tough choice. Do the personal work to become a leader of leaders or step aside. If you opt to become a leader of leaders then know it is a humbling journey demanding vulnerability, coaching and great personal growth. You will need the quiet strength to nourish, support and hold other leaders together. If you opt to pass the leadership baton, please do so with grace, celebrating all that God has achieved through you. To bring a community to this point is a phenomenal accomplishment.

The core work of the leader of leaders is influencing. That is deciding and bringing your influence to bear on key decisions, such as, is it time to consider a second edge-community in another location? The primary aim here is not growing big, but allowing your 'work' to mature and become a viable expression of gospel life to people in need, while also being visible so that centre-churches can observe. Influence can also happen through supporting other radical start-ups. How can you help them with ideas, encouragement and wise advice? You can influence centre-churches to catch on to the gospel innovation you have established and see how they could also learn and adapt this into their own contexts. Tell your story to other Christians to encourage their faith and mobilise them for mission.

As an established edge-community with a particular gospel focus, you can have influence in the wider community, taking what you have learnt into other community groups, local government and speciality services to further strengthen and improve allied work. The experiences and the lessons learnt are a gift to others. If no other organisation is working in the area you have developed, share your story so other charities, local communities, churches and government agencies can understand the need and seek to contribute. Edge communities that had done the years of hard work can bless society with their unique perspectives.

Influence by fostering new edge movements

Established edge-communities can multiply their influence by looking for other groups, new ventures and edge-leaders to champion, support or encourage. Perhaps becoming a mentor to an edge-leader who is starting out, or in a peer relationship that encourages you both and fosters new edge communities. Influencing can happen through starting or joining a movement of edge-communities. With an eye to how God could be seeking to reshape and refine the church, how can your community throw its weight and credibility behind a bigger movement? There is no specific answer to this question, but it is one that communities at this point need to grapple with in prayer and conversation.

Influencing the wider church

Recognise your gift and charism and make it available in the easiest way to the wider body of Christ so others can receive that gift and embody it in their own way. Be willing to tell your story in ways a global community can access: write a book, produce a podcast, start a blog, create video content of your edge-community life and the lessons you have learnt along the way. Get on social media and advocate for more groups like yours, more compassion for the people group you care for and greater commitment to following Jesus in the injustices and idolatries of our time.

Multiplying

Being established as an edge-community and in your charism opens opportunities for you to be strategic and plant more communities. This could mean planting another edge-community in a different location or growth within your existing edge-community.

Keep the main thing the main thing

Influence comes from the reality of the life God is bringing within your edge-community. Influence is not the primary focus; it is simply making everything count twice. Your first call is to be faithful to your charism. At the same time as you become an author, global podcaster or regular speaker at conferences and events, remember to keep your roots deep in your edge-community relationships and the life of your gospel renewal work. Don't become a disconnected guru telling old stories about a community that no longer exists or you are no longer committed to. Conference stages and bookshelves are already full of these.

Watch for mission drift

As you and your edge-community become recognised and your work acknowledged, there is a risk of becoming comfortable, or side-tracked. It is easy to lose some of your original commitment and vision. Justin regularly tells the story of the YMCA, who started off very Christian and lost their Christian core, what Jesus would call their 'saltiness', along the way. At this point you need to face tough questions:

❖ Are you still all in for the gospel?

❖ Are you and your community still passionately committed to Jesus?

❖ Are you practicing good discipleship and encouraging deep belonging?

❖ Is this leading to your community living out an embodied gospel imperative?

Many years ago, Justin heard Dave Andrews reflecting on what became of people he started out with in edge ministry. Dave's comment was "they started doing good and ended up doing very well or maybe even became a Bishop!" As our edge communities gain recognition, we can reach a point where we are prospering personally from our edge involvement and then it is very easy to stop being about what God called us to.

The risk on the edge is the more successful you become the more likely you are to be removed from your original charism. Robert Chambers in his book *Rural Poverty Unperceived*[15] makes the point that the more successful we are in life the more we are removed from relating to poverty. The natural directional flow of success is away from the places that most need us. The very success and recognition of edge communities will have a natural domesticating impact on them that has to be constantly worked against. Edge communities which used to be volunteer based become professionalized. Governance and management processes can easily take over. Due to the community's profile and success, leaders and community can become risk adverse and safety conscious. Ultimately, if this trajectory continues, they become another part of the centre. Because there is a tendency for the cutting nature of your commitment and edge-life to dull, in this season your community needs to seek renewal.

What the Centre does

As a centre-church leader, you are now in a dynamic and inspiring In-tensional relationship and ongoing conversation with an edge-community. This is an interdependent relationship between two established communities and leaderships, offering a wonderful learning context for centre-leaders and congregations. It is a source of encouragement and gospel stories as well as a challenge to the centre to see and learn from the edge. The centre church can observe the edge-community's charism and the resources and learnings that are present in their community life. Then centre-churches can adapt them for their context. We have seen edge charisms influencing centre-churches in the areas of liturgy, discipleship material, prayer practices and rhythms, missional strategies, and worship music.

The edge offers a lived example of a practical gospel faith that speaks to the need of a segment of the wider community. For many in centre-church this will be challenging. As the edge's white-hot, wholehearted faith, lived on the edge will call many in your church community to increase their own fidelity to Christ in a compromised and idolatrous world. The more you expose your centre-church community to edge faith, the more they will be encouraged and begin to sense alternative ways of being and living-out their own faith. Share podcasts and stories, invite the edge into the pulpit, encourage people to read key books and offer visits to meet with the edge-community in their spaces. Don't expect the edge to come to you. The onus is on the centre to walk the extra mile to build this meaningful relationship.

Centre-church, and especially their leaders need to consider what aspects of edge community may help the centre church realign. What gospel focus do these edge groups incarnate that may help us understand the deepest cultural angst of our time? Over the last 30 years the edge has embraced:

❖ A yearning for deep belonging and community

❖ Authenticity

❖ Discipleship

❖ Bicultural journey

❖ God's preferential bias for the poor

❖ Care of creation

Today many in centre-church leadership would say we recognise these things. Given that edge communities were leaning into these areas several decades ago, with some in-tensional relationship the centre church could have pivoted faster. In a rapidly changing world, we need to be more responsive to valuable learnings on our doorstep.

We need to create relationships between centre and edge that will lead to real transformation.

The in-tensional relationship you have built with an edge-community and its leaders provides a foundation for doing it again with a new group. Seeking answers to the following kind of questions will help.

- ❖ Where is God raising up new apostolic or prophetic leaders to a new gospel venture?

- ❖ How is this group shaping their life together?

- ❖ What societal angst they are responding to?

- ❖ What can you and your congregation learn from them?

- ❖ Can you translate what they are living into the life of the congregation?

- ❖ Imagine an edge-community made up several households who purposefully take in people on parole providing them a safe home, a stable community and life-on-life discipleship. Few in the centre-church congregation are likely to relocate and join this edge-community but they could be inspired to have people from the community around for a meal. That meal may encourage a second or third meal together, unearthing a shared interest with the person on parole, thus broadening their support networks and adding another Jesus follower to their lives.

Hopefully some of the commitment, holistic living and white-hot faith of the edge-dwellers is rubbing off on the congregation inspiring at least some into their own deeper, more costly expressions of life following Jesus. In this in-tensional relationship the edge's commitment and life is influencing and modelling renewal in the congregation.

Summary

❖ If an edge community manages to sustain and build a relationship with the centre church, it will often have an influence far greater than its own footprint. This could be:

- Increased influence in wider society

- Increased influence in wider church

- Increased opportunity to birth, mentor and support other edge groups.

- Multiplying more edge communities

❖ As edge communities increase in influence and potentially become 'successful', then beware. Edge communities can become domesticated and suffer missional drift.

❖ If a healthy in-tensional relationship has been built, the centre church can receive:

- Innovative resources

- Heat from the edge's contagious faith

- A better understanding of the deepest cultural angsts of our time.

Chapter 9 — In-tensional In Action

The stress test of any community is how they respond in a crisis. Alan, who was Senior pastor at South West Baptist Church for 12 years, saw this clearly in the aftermath of the devastating events of the 15th of March 2019.

"Our church, comprising both centre and edge elements, was rocked by the tragedy of a gunman targeting two Christchurch mosques, killing 51 people and wounding 40. It was a quiet Friday afternoon; I was sitting at home working on Sunday's sermons when a church member rang to say the wife of one of our sponsored refugee families had rung distraught and asking for a ride to the hospital. He was driving to meet her. A few minutes later the areas around the two mosques were surrounded by armed police. The city hospital was overrun, schools across the city were locked down and sirens screamed shrilly across the whole city.

The mother who had called for a ride to the hospital was outside the mosque. Her family was one of three refugee families that neighbourhood communities of the church had sponsored, providing support and care in the first two years of their time in New Zealand. At that time the church had eight such neighbourhood communities: our version of intentional mission communities focused on seeing the Kingdom of God nurtured in neighbourhoods.

While Christchurch had been rocked by numerous earthquakes a few years before, this attack was quite different. It took days for official information to come through. When it came it confirmed what we already knew from those who had been sitting with the families in the hospital. The woman who phoned for a ride to the hospital lost her husband and her oldest son. Both shot and killed in the attack. Her younger son was badly wounded. A father from another refugee family sponsored by a neighbourhood community was also badly wounded. The father of the third family we sponsored decided, at the last minute, not to go the mosque but rather to meet his friends later at the shopping mall. A simple decision with massive consequences. It was in the weeks following this tragic event that I was most proud of our church. Are you allowed to be proud of a church?

The eight neighbourhood communities, while edge-like in their rhythms, life and focus were strongly connected to the centre and equally part of the church. Three of these communities had sponsored a family; finding and equipping a home for them, guiding them through tax, banking, government financial support, school enrolments, medical and dental care and the basics of how to get by in New Zealand. Two other neighbourhood communities had formed deep links over a decade or more in their local, low decile schools and communities. They knew Muslim families in their patch and these families who were scared and anxious naturally turned to them in their fear and overwhelming grief.

The Sunday after the shooting, when we gathered the whole church for worship, there was an overwhelming feeling of sadness and sombre disbelief. This was Christchurch, sure we'd been rocked by natural disaster but not intentional evil. Attacks like this happened in other places, not our quiet garden city. We held our usual three services that day, and the mood was the same in all three. Standing up the front, I named those who had died, and I tried to name people's feelings, hold the depths of their pain and anger and point them to Jesus who also knew suffering and birthed hope. The church responded. Those with time offered it, those without dug deep into their wallets, hugs and tears flowed. At times like this it is very good to be part of such a church.

In the weeks that followed, the centre church was able to support those in neighbourhood communities who were the face-to-face support of those directly affected. Because most of those killed and wounded were men, and Muslim women have strict gender boundaries, it was the women of the neighbourhood communities who could go to grieving widows, sit with them in hospital and care for their children.

That week I attended a meeting of church leaders from across the city that was called in response to the tragedy. The whole city was reeling, and church leaders wanted to pray and to help. At that meeting of church leaders made up of all denominations and a variety of churches – Catholics and Pentecostals, Anglicans and Reformed, independents and house churches – I realised these deeply caring leaders lacked one thing that was at the forefront for us. Some spoke of people in their church who taught at schools where family members of pupils were lost, others of church members who had staff at their workplaces who were killed or injured or church members who worked at the hospital and were under enormous strain. These were real and significant connections, but primarily professional. At our church, because of the neighbourhood community investment, many people had personal friendships and trusted relationships with the Muslim families who were suffering. That was a unique connection and opportunity to care.

In the days that followed other organisations saw the connections and the work that our church was doing and gave significant financial support to enable us to provide the on the ground care that the families needed. Families were fed, necessary bills were paid, and two staff were employed by the church for six months to co-ordinate care, support the communities and advocate on their behalf. This meant the neighbourhood community people were supported from the centre to do the personal friendship-based care with the help of expertise and food, counselling services and guidance from professionals. Here's one story to illustrate.

One of the neighbourhood communities had years before begun a business as a hub for the area and to raise profits for global and local need. One of their local focuses is the nearby low decile, multi-cultural primary school. For years this neighbourhood community of the church had been supporting the school by providing volunteers to read, to help with sport and a team of skilled musicians to provide lessons. They'd served as school board members and subsidised directly or worked to raise extra curricula funding. The business worked with the school to build a whanau room, a place on the school grounds where parents could gather, drink coffee and chat. As timing would have it the whanau room was finished and furnished and the opening set for the Monday after the shooting. From day one it became a place for Muslim mums to gather. Amid the fear of more attacks, the vulnerability of being a Muslim on the street, and the grief of losing husbands and sons, this was a place where they felt safe. It was the women of the local neighbourhood community who could be with them, listening and re-assuring, and praying for them.

For me that was the power of a centre-edge church at work. For a decade I, as a centre church leader, had nurtured the growth of the edge while getting on with my day job leading centre-church life. During that time, I had carried an image that had come to me with clarity and conviction as I prayed one morning. The image was of a typical door hinge. Hinges have three components – two knuckles each with their leaf and a pin. The leaf is the flat metal plate with holes to anchor it to the door or the frame. The knuckle of each leaf is a line of round hoops which the knuckle of the second leaf slots into. Once together, the pin can slide through the knuckle holes creating the pivot point. In this image I saw my role as being the pin held tightly to both the centre and edge, enabling them to come together.

I was also a pin between the young change agents and the older church members, there since the wonderful growth of the 1970s and 80s, devotedly giving their lives to God's work through the church. For several years, I walked around with a hinge in my satchel. At stressful times when edge and centre or young and old were at odds, I put the hinge in my pocket as a reminder that I was to be like the pin between them. While this role was not easy it was rewarding. I made heaps of mistakes along the way. We made some silly decisions and backed some lame horses, but we saw glimpses of God bringing something new in the neighbourhood communities."

These edge-communities can inspire the centre-church with their commitment and passion. For example, one of the Urban Vision teams is passionate about their suburb's lack of public housing and the pressure it causes on the few available rentals. They identified some vacant council land where public housing once stood, but which had never been replaced, and mobilized their Urban Vision team, the church they attend and their wider neighbourhood into action. They set up a festive camping 'occupation', attracting media attention, and bringing the public's attention to the number of empty homes in the area. They highlighted the City Council's failure to prioritise making homes available, despite the housing crisis in their area.

Urban Vision knew and cared for those caught in this housing crisis and brought the stories of those living in overcrowded homes – or even cars and caravans – to the media, emphasising the way the local church was offering support. Through this they became a positive example and something of an advert for the God who cares for the dispossessed. For the wider community, their stance and action showed that the 'church' cared and got actively involved in local issues of injustice.

The powerful witness of God intervening tangibly in people's lives can grow the faith and imagination of the centre. Having caught a picture of the edge's alternative, lived reality, local congregations may take a little of that innovation and creativity and sow it their own congregational life. This may well see local neighbourhood churches renewed for another generation. We believe these edge communities and expressions of faith will be a transformative oasis offering a local alternative and hope to the deepest angst of our society.

Final thought from Justin

As we come to the end it feels right to talk about what I have experienced as I have attempted, over almost ten years, to follow my own advice. I will talk about my journey as Bishop of Wellington. A few disclaimers: firstly, in Aotearoa New Zealand, Māori have a saying, *Kāore te kūmara e kōrero mō tōna ake reka*. Which can be translated as 'the kūmara doesn't speak of its own sweetness'. It is a Māori way of saying don't talk yourself up. I have felt a constant tension in this book around appearing self-promoting and especially now as I turn to talk about the Wellington Diocese.

Secondly, any achievements feel small and fragile. I often say that I have seen different ministries "catch a wave" where they seem to have been incredibly fruitful and then their leaders write books and speak about their journey and they become famous in church circles. But most of us struggle to replicate their success. In my 30 years in ministry, I thank God (at least now I do, a younger me would have felt resentful) that I have never felt like I "caught a wave". Instead, I feel like I just faithfully laboured at the dreams God called Jenny and me to. Then after 5 or 10 years we would wake up exhausted and suddenly realise there was some fruit. I say this because the journey over the last nearly 10 years has been fruitful, but not in any sense spectacular. This is a good thing for me because I think the learnings are proven in and out of season.

Thirdly, I realise that churches or denominations are complex eco-systems. It's seldom the whole story when we say, "we did x and we got the following result". So, as I discuss what I think we are achieving I do not assume that this book's content is a direct correlation to the positive changes, however I think it has had far more impact than many realise.

Finally, I am aware than when we start talking about positive fruit there can be an inherent implied criticism of what has gone before. Therefore, the temptation is to say nothing out of love and respect to those who have faithfully given their life for God's church. Recognising this I feel that I honour them most by having this conversation because I to want to meet their love and courage to serve God's church the best I can.

This is what we've achieved by living into this in-tensional relationship between centre and edge

We have managed to dramatically transform the day-to-day culture across the diocese, and this is starting to permeate local congregations. This culture has the following traits:

❖ A move from individualism to recognition that it's not about any individual but about God.

❖ A move from individualism to recognition that it's not about any individual but about the body of Christ as expressed in a local context.

❖ A move from individualism to recognition that it's not about any individual but about those who are on the edges/margins and not present in our centre-midst.

❖ A culture that recognises that the church is primarily a volunteer movement where some may get paid.

❖ A culture where the ministry belongs to the body of believers not to the clergy.

❖ A culture where we make decisions according to what we think God is asking us to do, not on what we have money for. In ministry we do what we are called to do; "If it's worth doing its worth doing for free!"

❖ A culture that recognises form follows function, therefore structures are our servants and if they are not serving then they are not the structures we want.

❖ A culture that recognises that it's not structures that change the world but empowered faithful people.

❖ A culture that says renewal is not possible without an increase in spiritual temperature, commitment and repentance from idols.

I focus a lot on the culture changes first, because that is what I learnt on the edge for years. If you get the right culture everything else comes easier.

Practically we have experienced an influx of young adults; for a church that is known to be old and stagnant we have many vibrant, creative and committed younger people. We now have good pipelines for next generation leadership from both centre and edge. We have been able to move the conversation in numerous places from how to manage decline to how and who is going to replant/renew these communities. We have a growing cohort of younger leaders who will and are committed to going wherever God calls them, empowered by God regardless of whether the church can pay them. This is a phenomenal emerging strength.

We have been able to renew and replant numerous churches on basically no money, we have seen numerous marginal, fragile and dying churches flourish.

We now have many edge communities, most living in intentional, self-supporting residential community and each with a clear missional focus. At the beginning of each year, they covenant together: 200 people, most of younger generations. This is a miracle.

Over the years across the diocese, we have seen an increase in the daily office. Many groups – centre and edge – have a corporate daily prayer rhythm.

We have seen an increase in active justice-making across our diocese, with more people becoming aware of and involved in important justice issues of our time.

How have we done this? We attempted (badly) to do what we have written about here. We have actively taught into centre-edge sociology, attempting to give both edge and centre the language to understand the issues. We have normalised the tensions; they are not personal or about character flaws they are inherent sociological tensions. If we are experiencing them, it's a sign we are doing something right. The question is how to manage them appropriately.

The edge has criticised me for going soft. The centre has criticised me for being biased towards the edge. I have tried (on a good day) to defend both, speak well of both and teach others to do so.

I have deliberately been very protective of the edge, not wanting it to give the best of its energy to rescue a declining church. We need a healthy edge. On numerous occasions it would have been easy to load the edge down with centre management and governance, but their call would have paid the price. So instead, a few of us operate as sponsors, making sure management and governance works for the edge and is informed by it.

In the Diocese we have set up a separate container to support and mentor the edge so that different groups can be developed and supported and find their voice. In this structure the edge conversation can be the norm, without having to speak centre language. We have tried to find the points of influence and overlap where centre and edge can build mutually beneficial and supportive relationships without either group feeling overwhelmed.

I think a by-product of learning to live in this tension positively and creatively is that as a Diocese we can manage other positions of diversity as a strength.

This hasn't been easy. Personally, although I know this material incredibly well, studied into it for a PhD that died on becoming bishop, and have lived it for over 35 years, I still underestimate how hard it is to do.

Even after this journey and its fruit, I tend to refrain from talking about Urban Vision in an Anglican context. Over the years I have felt that the easiest way to dismiss the Bishop would be to say he wants to turn the Diocese into Urban Vision. So, I prefer to talk about the other edge groups in the Diocese. This has been sad for me personally but it's not personal. It's just a normal consequence of sociological tension!

The icing on the cake

On the 5th of August 2022, Bishop Eleanor Sanderson of Wellington Diocese stood up at Lambeth Conference to deliver part of a Plenary to approximately 1500 attendees.

Lambeth Conference is the global gathering of Anglican/ Episcopalian Bishops; it normally takes place every ten years, but with covid and other issues it had been 14 years since the last conference. The Anglican church is in over 160 countries (numbering about 85 million members) and many of these were represented: 650 Bishops attended with spouses. The Archbishop of Canterbury Justin Welby led the conference, navigating the communion regarding globally divisive issues of sexuality. As the strength of the communion lies outside of the West many of the voices taking the microphone were from contexts where the church is growing despite many hardships. Most Lambeth attendees were aware that the Western Anglican church was significantly struggling (as we identified in chapter 1).

It was surprising that Bishop Eleanor was given 25 minutes to talk about Discipleship, one of the few Western contexts to be profiled. Jenny and I sat, listened and watched as Eleanor told the story of discipleship and missional communities in the Wellington diocese primarily over the last 10 years. She talked about the multiplication of missional communities, the centrality of discipleship and the beginning of revitalising and renewing a declining and aging diocese (not to mention flabby, insipid, compromised and idolatrous, but we are great people!).

Jenny and I sat so proud of Eleanor and the stories she told of our wonderful friends who had poured their lives out over the last few years. At the end of her talk a third of the 1500 stood and gave her a standing ovation. The gathering of global bishops representing 85 million Anglicans, where the Western church is known to be struggling, chose to be influenced by the story of the Wellington Diocese.

The unrecognised core of that story was that many of the groups Eleanor profiled had been directly influenced by Urban Vision. The global Anglican church in the West chose to go to a far-flung country, to a relatively globally insignificant diocese in the heart of a secular culture, looking for hope, inspiration and innovation to help Western Anglicanism find a way forward. Underpinning the stories Eleanor told was a small group of followers, who for years had relocated to marginalised neighbourhoods and joined in God's transforming work there.

As I sat there that day, I realised that what I was witnessing was the tip of the iceberg of influence, and the message of this book lived out.

Conclusion

This book is based on a conversation between prophetic edge leaders and centre leaders. A conversation that will need intentionality from both sides as inevitable tension arises. These in-tensional relationships are the change dynamic that God has used throughout history.

In countries like New Zealand where churches are rapidly shrinking, with aging buildings to maintain, rising costs of compliance and smaller congregations to bear the load and pay for the pastor or vicar; the heart and work of edge-dwellers can be refreshing and inspiring. They drag us back to a whole of life costly calling and a can-do attitude.

We believe that God continues to raise up pioneering communities that intuitively respond to the deepest cultural angst of our times. These communities are small and fragile, yet they are a wonderful gift of the Spirit. These communities offer the possibility of change where church leaders haven't been able to bring it. Deep down we know that society needs this kind of renewed expression of the gospel. For centre-church these edge communities offer a path into the unknown and, to quote scripture, they are a light to our path. We pray that this book will encourage and enable in-tensional conversations, producing churches that are able to engage the needs and longings of society with the deep truths, life, healing and hope of the Lord Jesus Christ.

Notes and References

1 Tensional is also a rare technical term in linguistics and logic.

2 What we have called the 'edge-centre dynamic of church life' has been rigorously researched, under various labels, by scholars like Ernest Troeltsch and H. Richard Niebuhr, Stark & Bainbridge and Finke & Stark. For a summary of this enduring model, explaining the rise and fall of religious movements a useful text is – 'Organizational Revival from Within: Explaining Revivalism and Reform in the Roman Catholic Church' by Roger Finke and Patricia Wittberg in *The Journal for the Scientific Study of Religion. Vol 39, Issue 2; June 2000 (pages 154-170).*

Useful texts include:

- *Creating A Future For Religious Life: A Sociological Perspective* (1991) Wittberg, Patricia S.C.; Paulist Press: New York.

- *Pathways to Re-Creating Religious Communities* (1996) Wittberg, Patricia S.C.; Paulist Press: New York.

- *The Rise and Fall of Catholic Religious Orders: A Social Movement Perspective* (1994) Wittberg, Patricia S.C.; The State University of New York Press: New York.

3 Ralph Winter was Professor of Missions at the School of World Mission at Fuller Theological Seminary. For a summary of his work on modalities and sodalities see 'The Two Structures of God's Redemptive Mission' in *Perspectives on the World Christian Movement: A Reader* (1981) Edited by Ralph D. Winter & Steven C. Hawthorne: William Carey Library; Pasadena. (p178-190).

4 George Ling describes modality and sodality saying "*modality* comes from the root word *mode*. This in turn refers to the customary way things are done… *Sodality* comes from the Latin root, *Sodalis*. This can be translated comrade, or using other words, all of which suggest closeness and active partnership: companion, associate, mate, crony, accomplice, conspirator are all listed. *Sodalitas* was used for social and politics associations; religious fraternities; electioneering gangs and guilds… one crude interpretation of a difference between modality and sodality, (*is*) that the modal is people-centred and the sodal is task-centred. That is not the heart of it as sodal groups are classically, and uncharacteristically, highly committed to one another, although completing a given task is cardinal in sodal identity." See: https://c4so.org/wp-content/uploads/2022/06/Lings-Why-Modality-and-Sodality-thinking-is-vital-to-understand-future-church.pdf

5 Winter taught that both need the other. George Ling adds "It is not good for modal to be alone – one might say." See: https://c4so.org/wp-content/uploads/2022/06/Lings-Why-Modality-and-Sodality-thinking-is-vital-to-understand-future-church.pdf

6 Moore, Robert L. (2003) *Facing the Dragon: Confronting Personal and Spiritual Grandiosity*. Chiron; Wilmette.

7 Ganss, George (1992) *The Spiritual Exercises of Saint Ignatius* p32.

8 *Wayfinding Leadership: Ground Breaking Wisdom For Developing Leaders* (2015) by Spiller, C; Barclay-Kerr, H; & Panoho, J.; Huia Publishers: Wellington

9 See: https://c4so.org/wp-content/uploads/2022/06/Lings-Why-Modality-and-Sodality-thinking-is-vital-to-understand-future-church.pdf for full quote. A Walls, *The Missionary Movement in Christian History*, (Edinburgh: T&T Clark, 1996) pp. 16-25.

10 Friedrich-Silber, *Virtuosity, Charisma, and Social Order: A Comparative Sociological Study of Monasticism in Theravada Buddhism and Medieval Catholicism*, p154.

11 *The Rise and Fall of Catholic Religious Orders: A Social Movement Perspective* (1994) Wittberg, Patricia S.C.; The State University of New York Press: New York. p144

12 George Ling states: "New Testament evidence and recent research shows that modal (*centre*) church needs to affirm and recognise its pioneers as sodal (*edge*) church who should be expected to do things differently. It would be possible to explore the church criticism experienced by Peter after his visit to Cornelius, or Paul's treatment at the hand of Judaisers for biblical warrant. My colleague Beth Keith has recently shown, mainly from Anglican patterns of deployment, that often we are getting it wrong in the way we use pioneers (*we'd call edge leaders*). Those sent to modal (*centre*) contexts, or to do a bit of sodal (*edge*) in the midst of modal (*centre*), are frustrated by the system, always explaining themselves to authorities, less able ro envisage what is needed, and to establish why any may nevertheless begin. Those liberated into sodal (*edge*) contexts are free to re-imagine what is needed, glad to be accountable but not controlled, and able to start what is easier to sustain." Brackets added. See: https://c4so.org/wp-content/uploads/2022/06/Lings-Why-Modality-and-Sodality-thinking-is-vital-to-understand-future-church.pdf

13 Patricia Wittberg, S.C. (1996) *Pathways to Re-Creating Religious Communities.* Paulist Press: New York page 199-200

14 See: https://c4so.org/wp-content/uploads/2022/06/Lings-Why-Modality-and-Sodality-thinking-is-vital-to-understand-future-church.pdf

15 (1983).

About the Authors

Alan and Justin have known each other for a quarter of a century in various capacities in church leadership.

Justin was elected Archbishop Tikanga Pakeha of the Anglican Church in Aotearoa, New Zealand and Polynesia in May 2024, having served as Bishop of Wellington since 2012, during which time his passion has been for the renewing of Jesus' church; most often through the interplay of centre and edge expressions. He is the co-founder of Urban Vision, a movement of local residential intentional communities which seek to serve those at the margins of their neighbourhoods. Justin is married to Jenny, and lives in Whanganui. He is father to the marvellous Luca, Jesse and Maya.

Justin and Jenny have also co-published *Against the Tide, Towards the Kingdom* (Eugene, Oregon: Wipf and Stock, 2011).

Alan has been an Aotearoa New Zealand pastor for 30 years. He has is also sociologist who has researched faith development. He is married to Sandra and lives in Ōtautahi Christchurch close to their children and four grandchildren. He has written four prior books:

- *A Churchless Faith*, (Philip Garside Publishing Ltd, New Zealand, 2000). Published internationally by SPCK, 2002.

- *Called Again*, (Philip Garside Publishing Ltd in NZ, 2004.) Retitled and published internationally as, *Journeying in Faith,* by SPCK, 2004.

- *Five Years On*, (Portland Research Trust, New Zealand 2006. Published internationally by SPCK under the title, *Church Leaving*, 2006.

- *Chrysalis: The hidden transformation in the journey of faith*, (2008, Carlisle: Paternoster). Republished in French as *Chrysalide: les Metamorphoses de la foi*, 2016.

You can email the authors here:

Justin: justin.ngatiawa@gmail.com

Alan: aj@portland.org.nz

www.ingramcontent.com/pod-product-compliance
Lightning Source LLC
Chambersburg PA
CBHW021651120626
46545CB00002B/809